Resolving Conflict in Africa

The Fermeda Workshop

RESOLVING

CONFLICT

IN AFRICA

THE FERMEDA WORKSHOP

Leonard W. Doob, editor
William J. Crockett
Yousuf Jama Ali Duhul
Andreas Eshete
Charles K. Ferguson
William J. Foltz
John J. Okumu
Robert B. Stevens
Richard E. Walton
Thomas A. Wickes

New Haven and London, Yale University Press, 1970

Library of Congress catalog card number: 71-123396
International standard book number: 0-300-01375-2 (clothbound);
0-300-01376-0 (paperbound)
Designed by Sally Sullivan,
set in IBM Selectric Press Roman type,
and printed in the United States of America by
The Carl Purington Rollins Printing-Office
of the Yale University Press.
Distributed in Great Britain, Europe, and Africa by
Yale University Press, Ltd., London; in Canada by
McGill-Queen's University Press, Montreal; in Mexico
by Centro Interamericano de Libros Académicos,
Mexico City; in Australasia by Australia and New
Zealand Book Co., Pty., Ltd., Artarmon, New South
Wales; in India by UBS Publishers' Distributors Pvt.,
Ltd., Delhi; in Japan by John Weatherhill, Inc.,
Tokyo.

To the many Africans
and other friends
this Wild Idea
has had
and still needs
everywhere

Contents

Preface

During the first two weeks of August 1969 a group of Africans and Americans came together in a South Tyrolean hotel called the Fermeda in order to determine whether they might contribute to the solution of two costly, misery-producing border disputes in the Horn of Africa. The conflicts are between Ethiopia and Somalia and between Kenya and Somalia. In the recent past people have been killed during clashes between Somali nomads and the police or soldiers of Kenya and Ethiopia; and an occasional death from this same cause continues to be reported even now. The Africans did not officially represent their countries—Fermeda was not a summit meeting—and therefore could not commit their foreign offices to any kind of policy or decision. The objective of the project, therefore, was to ascertain whether in the detached and permissive atmosphere of a workshop the participants might express and then modify some of their attitudes and values, improve their communication skills, reveal the deeper psychological or emotional issues in the disputes, and thus move closer to an innovative resolution. This book describes and evaluates what happened.

Any solution or hint of a solution in such an atmosphere obviously would be achieved in the absence of the constraints placed upon diplomats in real life and could therefore remain pure fantasy. For practical reasons, we quickly add, we have also been interested in discovering whether the influential elite who gathered at Fermeda would or could transmit their new knowledge and insight to the leaders in authority. Then we realize that these conflicts in the Horn of Africa, tragic and wasteful as they are to the three countries, do not loom large in present-day world perspective. Any contribution to the technique of resolving conflict in one situation, however, is likely to be useful more generally in international negotiations and diplomacy. In short, we appreciate full well the gap between Fermeda and the real world, and we acknowledge that the problems of the Horn are not exactly like those in other disputes. We assert, nevertheless, that Fermeda might at the very least initiate ideas that potentially can have practical, widespread repercussions.

The immediate methodological aim of the workshop was to gain what might be called clinical experience in the use of a technique called sensitivity training. That technique involves a prolonged series of small-group sessions that are unstructured so far as procedure is concerned, thus placing a premium upon relatively free expression of feelings and interaction; through them it is hoped that the participants will gain greater self-knowledge and will learn to communicate their views more effectively than is the case in most formal meetings. The groups are frequently called T-groups (T for training), and the permissive leaders are known as trainers. At Fermeda we were not testing the validity of this technique in any ultimate way. We were merely utilizing it to try to create an atmosphere in which international discord might be better understood and eventually diminished. We did not, we do not, believe that sensitivity training is a panacea; rather, in our opinion it is a technique that should be assayed and modified for the purpose at hand. Obviously more experience of this sort is needed.

At Fermeda there were six Africans from each of the three countries; four professional trainers, all Americans; three of us from Yale University, also Americans;

an executive assistant, an American woman; and, toward the very end of the period, an American observer. The workshop was not conducted in Africa because we all thought it wiser to meet at a neutral site; and the South Tyrol qualified.

As the reader moves from chapter to chapter in this book, he will easily discover that each contributor is reacting to a different part of the elephant. The African scholars are less than enthusiastic concerning the accomplishments of Fermeda; the trainers also express reservations, but by and large they believe their technique was at least partially successful; and my colleagues and I waver between the two extremes. In order to communicate what we learned, we have provided the raw data, however contradictory and repetitious they may appear.

A word about how this book was written. Two years before Fermeda I published a chapter in a book in which I described the proposal and moaned that we could not execute it; some of that material has been incorporated into Chapter 1. Three months after Fermeda the three of us from Yale published our impressions of the workshop in a scholarly journal; a long section of that article has been used in Chapter 6 in this book. The most important fact to record here is that the three African contributors did not see our article until they had written their own chapters. We told them to say whatever they wished—and not to be polite about it. We did not influence them in any way. One factual and one theoretical point were raised with Mr. Okumu after he submitted his first draft, as a result of which he made a few minor changes in the manuscript. With this exception, the Africans have said exactly what they think —as should be self-evident when their words are read.

They will see each other's contribution for the first time when this book is published.

The four trainers had criticized a draft of our article before publication, and they had access to the printed version when it appeared. We also told them to write as they pleased. To reduce duplication, some of them exchanged comments and drafts of their manuscripts. Again the reader will note that each of them chose to describe the elephant somewhat differently.

The principle behind my editing has been to do as little as possible. Except for a very few unidiomatic or unclear words and phrases (not sentences, be it noted), the original manuscripts of the Africans have not been touched. The four trainers have been dealt with harshly: whole sentences, paragraphs, and even pages have been slashed in order to avoid excessive repetition because, perforce, men from the same profession inevitably noticed the same parts of the beast. In two instances elaborations have been relegated to appendices. I ask their pardon. An effort has been made, too, to delete as much jargon as possible—unsuccessfully, no doubt.

Since each contributor has presented his own account of Fermeda, and since each has somewhat unique credentials, the reader will note marked differences in style. Two of the African contributors write and think in an academic tradition, undoubtedly because they are currently attached to academic institutions:

Andreas Eshete (Ethiopia): Acting Instructor of Philosophy, Yale University

John J. Okumu (Kenya): Senior Lecturer in Political Science, University College, Nairobi

The third African is not from a university:

Yousuf Jama Ali Duhul (Somalia): practicing lawyer in Mogadiscio and former editor of a monthly magazine

The four trainers are very active practitioners; two have appointments in academic institutions and also frequently organize and conduct workshops for business enterprises and other institutions:

William J. Crockett: Vice President for Human Relations, Saga Administrative Corporation

Charles K. Ferguson: Chairman, Department of Conferences and Program Consultation, University of California at Los Angeles

Richard E. Walton: Professor of Business Administration, Harvard University

Thomas A. Wickes: Director of Personnel Development, TRW, Inc.

The three of us from Yale University hold academic posts in different fields: Foltz, political science; Stevens, law; and I, psychology. Prior to Fermeda none of us had had previous experience with workshops; all three had prolonged contact with Africa as teachers and researchers; Stevens, moreover, has been a legal consultant to various governments in Africa.

The structure of the book can be briefly outlined. Chapter 1 contains background material on the disputes between the countries, the workshop technique, and the vicissitudes that kind and nasty persons made us endure before we could assemble at Fermeda. Chapter 2 (with additional facts in Appendix 2) provides the first historical account of workshops in Africa and thereby suggests that this technique from the West can be transferred to another continent; it concludes by offering two charts listing the daily activities at Fermeda hour by hour. In the next four chapters (3 through 6) the participants evaluate the elephant, especially with reference to the substantive issues involved in the two conflicts. The three Africans make it perfectly clear how they feel about the workshop—as already indicated, their enthusiasm is more than restrained—and two of them clearly defend their own nation's right to the territory in dispute. The Yale trio participated in the workshop while simultaneously observing its emotional and intellectual struggles; our chapter concludes this section of the book.

The trainers next examine the beast in terms of the tradition of their craft. Both Chapter 7 and Chapter 8 are audits directed to the future: they seek not only to indicate and account for the successes and failures of the workshop, but also to emphasize procedural improvements that might be made in the future. An important point, the difference between workshops and conventional public international meetings, receives elaboration in Appendix 3. Finally, Chapter 9 suggests a way of approaching the resolution of the conflicts that derives its inspiration from the basic attitudes and values expressed by the eighteen Africans at Fermeda.

What was accomplished at Fermeda over and beyond the proposal contained in Chapter 9? At this writing it is still too early to tell whether any of the ideas the participants and we acquired through two weeks of interaction have diffused effectively to the governments. We do know that one or more of the African participants in each country have been debriefed, as one says these days, by their foreign offices and other government agencies. Perhaps on this level the ideas will diffuse farther—and yet, because such matters are secret, we may never know whether or not we have made a contribution to decisions reached by leaders and other policy makers.

Events in the meantime complicate whatever repercussions, favorable or otherwise, might have resulted from Fermeda. In October 1969 there was a coup d'etat in Somalia: among many other changes (including the assassination of the president and the jailing of the prime minister, who first supported Fermeda, then withdrew his support, and finally gave his approval), two of our participants have become very important ministers in the new government and two others have been members of a committee revising the country's constitution. There has been serious trouble in Haile Sellassie I University, to which most of our Ethiopian scholars are attached. Kenya is peaceful, but all the consequences of Tom Mboya's assassination are not yet visible. Under these circumstances the isolation of Fermeda's contribution will remain a tricky challenge.

Throughout this book all of us confess our mistakes—the biggest blunder of all, I modestly think, was committed by me when I invited one particular African to Fermeda (see Appendix 1)—because we want the experience to be utilized elsewhere. Since our return from the South Tyrol we have been in contact with various groups that seek some kind of similar innovation in resolving their own conflicts and therefore express interest in Fermeda. The United Nations Institute of Training and Research continues to encourage us. Thus outside of Africa the idea may also be diffusing, however slowly.

The list of persons to whom my Yale colleagues and I wish to express gratitude in an enterprise of this kind is necessarily very long. Some, especially those connected with governments, must, alas, remain nameless as, here at least, must the African participants except for the three who have courageously accepted our invitation to contribute to this book. For encouragement and for financial support we thank the following: the Academy for Educational Development (Alvin C. Eurich, Director, and Edward W. Barrett, who is responsible for the Academy's International Mediation Study); the Honorable W. Averell Harriman; the James Marshall Fund; and, above all, the Concilium on International Studies of Yale University (Joseph M. Goldsen, Executive Director, who eventually convinced himself that the project had scholarly as well as practical implications). Oscar Schachter of UNITAR, as well as Chief S. O. Adebo, who is Director of that United Nations agency, provided both the moral and the institutional support that was absolutely essential and invaluable. E. A. Bayne of the American Universities Field Staff in Rome originally directed our attention to the problems of the Horn and, together with Joan S. P. Curtiss in his office, provided generous advice and logistical support. Mr. Bayne's additional claim to immortality rests on the fact that he introduced us to Miss Sonya Haddad who then functioned efficiently, warmly, and cheerfully as secretary and house sister at Fermeda. Sheila L. Meyers kept our machinery in New Haven humming. Two American friends, James C. N. Paul in Addis Ababa and James S. Coleman in Nairobi, transmuted some of the misery produced by launching the project into a pleasing delight. Chester Kerr, Director of the Yale University Press, convinced us that we ought to collect chapters for this volume and that inclusion in the Yale Fastback Series would set the correct unpretentious tone we sought for our Idea-in-progress. Jane G. Olejarczyk, as always, has attended to the details of preparing the manuscript more promptly and elegantly than I deserve. We acknowledge permission from the Regents of the State of California and from The Journal Press to utilize, respectively, in Chapters 1 and 6, sections of reports by us which they have published and to which they hold

the copyright. Otherwise we are sorely tempted to heap
scorn and abuse on various villains on the East coast of
the United States who for selfish and selfless reasons
either prevented the workshop from taking place sooner
or hindered our efforts when they might have been helpful. We forgive them, perhaps, and render thanks to
Dame Fortune and our own constitutions for enabling
us to explore the possibilities inherent in a Wild Idea.

L. W. D.

New Haven, Connecticut
March 3, 1970

1. Planning the Workshop

by Leonard W. Doob

On the evening of August 1, 1969, a group of Africans and Americans boarded a hired "pullman" bus at the Rome airport. The Africans from Somalia and Ethiopia had just arrived after a long flight; those from Kenya had been in Rome for more than a day. The only woman was an American, an executive secretary. When everyone was seated, I made a very short welcoming speech that began by saying that it seemed as if only a miracle had brought us all together. The bus trip during the night and the next morning lasted over thirteen hours and brought us to an isolated, comfortable ski hotel far above the town of Bressanone (Brixen) in the South Tyrol of Northern Italy; it is named Fermeda (a Ladin word meaning "gorge") after a section of a range of majestic Dolomites visible beyond the wooded mountains in the foreground. There, when not participating in a workshop, all of us could sleep, eat, drink, walk, view the beautiful scenery, and—for those who knew Italian or German or used the language of gestures or love— converse or play with the handful of other guests.

The objective of the workshop that was to last almost two weeks was known to all the participants: to determine whether in idyllic surroundings it might be possible for men of good will to evolve a solution for unresolved border disputes that have produced the misery associated with war and the preparation for war. We— the three Americans from Yale University who organized the workshop—had other related motives, which we never concealed. As social scientists we wished to observe whether a particular technique, a version of

sensitivity training, might be helpful in bringing about a
resolution of the conflicts. Again and again in the planning stage I kept repeating to anyone who would listen
and to myself an oversimplified analogy I borrowed
from a forgotten source. If one person wants a window
in this room open and another person wants it shut, and
if they keep phrasing their desires in terms of the window, one of them must win and the other must lose, or
there will be some sort of only partially satisfactory
compromise. But if it can be discovered that the first
person really wants fresh air and the second seeks only
to avoid a draft, a creative solution may be possible:
opening the door or a window in another room could
provide fresh air without a draft. Would it be possible,
then, to provide a setting in which our African friends
might move a step or two closer to a solution for their
conflicts by probing beneath the surface demands for
territory? At a minimum both Africans and Americans
might secure new insights into the attitudes and values
behind the disputes. We also had personal reasons for
promoting the enterprise: we are deeply attached to
Africans and African countries; we would repay them
for the privilege of having been allowed to conduct research in their midst over the years; and of course—like
almost everyone else—we detest war.

The Border Disputes

I shall give only the main outline of the disputes between Ethiopia and Somalia and between Kenya and
Somalia. No description can possibly be considered
complete or impartial from the viewpoint of all the
antagonists. A footnote offers a set of references in
which the contentions of the three countries appear.[1] In

addition, the three African scholars in this volume have considered historical questions in their own chapters.

The Republic of Somalia, composed of what were formerly Italian and British Somaliland, achieved independence in 1960. The nation, unlike any other sub-Saharan country, is virtually homogeneous, for almost all its inhabitants can be said to belong to a Somali culture, loosely defined, and to speak essentially the same language.[2] For reasons varying from the historical and nationalistic to the humane and the political, Somalia seeks to "unite all those Somalis now living in French Somaliland, the Ogaden and other Somali-inhabited areas of Ethiopia, and in the Northern Frontier Territories of Kenya."[3] French Somaliland does not enter directly into the disputes being discussed here except that its ultimate status is obviously of practical and symbolic importance to Ethiopia, since, among other things, Djibouti, its capital, is the terminus of the railway line from Addis Ababa and hence that country's only outlet to the sea.

The areas in dispute are the Ogaden, the Haud, and the North Eastern Province of Kenya (formerly called the Northern Frontier District). According to the Somali definition, people of Somali culture—Somalis—are in the majority in both places. It is certain that bands of Somali nomads use the areas as grazing lands for their herds and that far greater numbers move back and forth into territory held by Ethiopia than that held by Kenya. Armed conflict breaks out from time to time along the borders and inside the territories, small numbers of men are killed, and all three countries spend a not inconsiderable part of their budgets in defensive or offensive operations by their police and military forces. Here an effort will be made—impartially, it is hoped—to summarize directly the arguments and counterarguments employed by leaders of the three countries in their own mass media and at international conferences.

Somalia

1. Most inhabitants of the two areas are our brothers, they are our kinsmen, they should join us. The only reason they are now separated from our nation is that these lands were given to Ethiopia and Kenya by the colonial powers.

2. Let the people in the two areas decide their own destiny; undoubtedly, since they are Somalis, they will decide to join us; an impartial investigation by the British in 1962 clearly showed that five of the six districts of the North Eastern Province wished to become part of Somalia and to leave Kenya.

3. We need the areas for our nomadic people, whose herds must move freely back and forth across the present borders according to the seasonal availability of water and grazing land; and perhaps oil will be discovered in the North Eastern Province.

4. Ethiopia and Kenya are acting like imperialists—black imperialists—when they prevent these lands from being given the opportunity to be reunited with us.

Ethiopia

1. We have legal and historical rights to occupy the lands we now control: our boundaries were established with the Italians for their part of Somalia according to various treaties, especially those of 1897 and 1908, and with the British for their part, also according to various treaties, particularly that of 1897; like Eritrea (now part

of Ethiopia), the Ogaden and the Haud as well as most of Somalia are lost provinces that belonged to us in ancient times.

2. Ethiopia is an independent, multiracial state, and nationality need not be determined by language or culture (for example, the German-speaking Swiss are not part of Germany); the Somalis in the Ogaden and the Haud are our people; we treat them well, they live happily with us, they intermarry with neighbors in our country.

3. The areas are important to us economically; if only Somalia would cooperate with us, we could arrange mutually beneficial economic pacts, since for purely geographical reasons our two countries are interdependent.

4. The Somalis are a threat to our security: they send into those lands troublemakers disguised as nomads; their own government is receiving military supplies from, and training in, the Soviet Union.

Kenya

1. Kenya also is a multiracial state in which different peoples live in harmony with one another; we cannot begin to give away our territory (especially the North Eastern Province, which is more than one-half our land area), for then our entire nation could be dismembered; just as the occupation of the White Highlands of Kenya by European settlers did not make that area British, so the presence of Somalis in the North Eastern Province does not justify Somalia's claim to its sovereignty.

2. If the Somalis living in the North Eastern Province wish to join Somalia, let them cross the frontier and do so—nobody is stopping them; if they remain, we shall

continue to treat them as our brothers, as indeed we treat all Africans.

3. The British created the idea of Greater Somalia in the first place and stirred up trouble in the North Eastern Province in accordance with their policy of divide and rule; they dispatched a commission to investigate public opinion in this area that was not theirs to evaluate or to give away and that is of economic importance to us.

4. Somalia has created trouble in the North Eastern Province through the Somali *shifta* [a word coming from the English "shifter," which has now acquired the connotation of bandit] who have infiltrated the area, and broadcasts from Radio Mogadiscio have tried to cause unrest inside our country; the Somalis are endangering Pan-African solidarity by appealing to tribal and religious interests.

If anyone unfamiliar with these two conflicts finds that the contentions and countercontentions have a familiar sound, he is not suffering from the illusion of déjà-vu: most of them are part of the litany or syndrome of nationalism anywhere and hence have a transnational character;[4] and they illustrate the classic conflict between the cattleman and the farmer. Sometimes the arguments are within the same frame of reference as those of the opposition, oftentimes they are not. Here, therefore, seem to be situations in which both sides agree on the basic economic and anthropological facts but disagree concerning the historical, political, and psychological interpretation to be placed upon those facts.

The Need for a New Approach

The conflict between the nomadic tradition of the Somalis and the fixed boundaries based on the colonial tradition have kept the Horn of Eastern Africa in a state of war or near war for almost a generation. Efforts have been made to resolve the border disputes through diplomacy and the good offices of the United Nations and the Organization of African Unity ever since Somalia's independence, but so far without permanent success. In May 1961 the African governments at the Monrovia Conference called upon Ethiopia and Somalia to settle their differences; in August 1963 representatives of Britain, Kenya, and Somalia met in Rome and tried without success to reach an agreement concerning the North Eastern Province; during 1964 the conflicts were discussed at Dar es Salaam, Lagos, and Cairo meetings of the Organization of African Unity, and resolutions calling upon the countries to settle their disputes peacefully were passed, again quite fruitlessly. At Accra in 1965 Ethiopia and Somalia agreed to refrain from hostile propaganda against each other; during that same year a series of meetings between Somalia and Kenya, largely instigated by President Nyerere of Tanzania, ended in a deadlock, and serious guerrilla warfare broke out in the disputed area. In the autumn of 1967, however, with moral encouragement from Presidents Nyerere and Obote of Uganda, and especially through the active intervention and mediation of President Kaunda of Zambia, first at an OAU meeting of the heads of state in Kinshasa and then at a special conference in Arusha, a detente was achieved by Kenya and Somalia that eventually involved trade, regulation of propaganda, diplomatic relations, and the expression of good intentions, but not the disputed territories as such. At the Kinshasa meeting there were also declarations of good will between Ethiopia and Somalia; in addition, a tenuous arrangement between the two countries has come into existence for settling specific difficulties in the disputed areas after they have arisen.

Direct negotiation, in short, has made little progress. The leaders of the three countries realize that the prospects for improvement in the future are not bright. They cannot, moreover, turn for inspiration to other parts of Africa. Since World War II, and especially since the attainment of independence, African states have been almost uniformly unsuccessful in carrying on negotiations among themselves. Certainly without exception the trend has been away from federation or the unification of the separate African states, as is exemplified by the failures of the Mali Federation,[5] Ghana and Guinea,[6] the Federation of Rhodesia and Nyasaland (a special problem, of course) and the difficulties of the three countries in East Africa (Uganda, Kenya, Tanzania—with the strange case of Zanzibar also involved) in trying to retain the bare minimum of their common services.[7] In these instances available records suggest (but do not prove) that African leaders have been operating in a manner that does not permit them to change their basic sentiments or political positions.

African political leaders, like their counterparts elsewhere, usually arrive at a meeting with stated goals. They follow fairly strict agenda that compel them to discuss issues in terms of surface demands and claims. During negotiations they are conscious of the fact that they will be compelled to issue public statements concerning the accomplishments of the meeting. They are never permitted to forget that they are responsible to the governments and peoples they represent. Under these circumstances, how can they possibly think freely or, if the word be permitted again, creatively? In passing, it is impossible to repress the conviction that this

African elite, whose members successfully rebelled against the West and who seek, whenever possible, to solve their own problems in an African manner, are themselves victims of Western procedures in the area of diplomacy, summit meetings, and all the communication trappings of conflict in the modern world; they ape too well the world from which they have ostensibly liberated themselves.

The Workshop as a Technique

In April 1966 officials of one of the countries in East Africa approached us at Yale University through Mr. E. A. Bayne of the American Universities Field service; they suggested that we organize a research team to investigate the feasibility of a federation of the East African Horn. Two of us, Stevens and I, discussed the request with some of our colleagues and rejected it: the research seemed too policy-oriented and too unrealistic, and we suspected that the basic data were already available. During one of our conversations the idea of the workshop arose as a technique that might be used to facilitate fruitful discussion about the border disputes. At this point the advice and sagacity of another colleague, Chris Argyris, who is an experienced trainer, proved most helpful.

Why did we hit upon the workshop as the technique? At the time—I say in self-defense—workshops, T-groups, and sensitivity training had not become the fad they now are in certain circles. None of us had actually participated in a workshop, but I had heard and read about them fairly extensively. I knew that a typical workshop consists of a number of persons, motivated by some problem usually connected with their work, who come together, often at an isolated site, for a period of a week or more and there under the supervision of trained experts learn about themselves and their difficulties in large part from one another. Frequent opportunities are deliberately provided for the participants, who for this purpose are subdivided into smaller groups of around a dozen persons (called T-groups, T for training), to experience most varied, intensely emotional, and very frank interaction. Conventional means for disseminating information, such as lectures and films, may supplement the group learning situations. Over a protracted period, therefore, virtually every hour of the day in this temporary community is allocated to activities more or less focused—though often in an unfocused manner—upon the problem at hand.

Workshops have been employed in the West by industries, laboratories, and other institutions to improve their own functioning; more recently, government has seized upon the approach in an attempt to make key personnel more sensitive to some of their own leadership problems. The most famous workshop—held during the summer at Bethel, Maine—has trained heterogeneous people who have been attracted for reasons as diverse, and as pure or as impure, as those that lead patients into psychoanalysis. At first workshops appeared in the countries of origin, the United States and Great Britain, but more recently they have diffused to other European countries and also to Latin America, India, and Japan. Most important of all, they had been employed with little or no modification in a number of African countries; I was acquainted with many but not with all the historical details presented both in the next chapter and in Appendix 2. Here, then, was a technique that could be transported from Western society to Africa.

I also felt at the time that the workshop as such had certain advantages as a learning experience. It provides an opportunity for individuals to have close and prolonged contact with one another and thus, minimally, at least to perceive diverse viewpoints. It offers a stimulating and intense experience in which the participants learn more about themselves, about their relations to other persons, and hence about their own behavior and roles in real life. It has at its disposal a variety of techniques promoting learning, such as lectures, role playing, exercises, and brainstorming. It virtually guarantees immediate "feedback" through prolonged contact in the face-to-face situation. It releases members of an organization or institution from many normal restraints by isolating them from their customary environment and, in a relatively unstructured setting, by encouraging them to express themselves. It enables them to work on problems that can conceivably be transferred to real-life situations. In Chapters 7 and 8 the Fermeda trainers provide a fair sample of how the more restrained members of their profession appraise the technique, and in 1966 I perceived their type of enthusiasm in what I read and heard.

My two Yale colleagues and I, in short, became cautiously convinced that the workshop might well serve the function of helping African scholars from the three countries to communicate effectively with one another, to burst through the verbal façades of the disputes, and perhaps to arrive at a creative solution. But being academic people, we were also skeptical; thus at the time I wrote:

Alas, the subject of workshops in general cannot be ended without striking a sour note as the devil's advocate. Every single statement concerning the glorious learning opportunities provided by the technique can be ripped into and twisted in such a way as to suggest that indeed learning is impeded by the workshop. Obviously, for example, the technique enables people to have contact, but just as obviously that experience can produce an unfavorable impression. People perceive one another, yes, but they may do so selectively: they hear only what they wish to hear. What has been called a mote-beam mechanism (perceiving traits in others which we do not perceive in ourselves) can operate to produce estrangement in a small group. Proactive and retroactive inhibitions can, respectively, prevent or blot out the necessary learning. Too much or too little anxiety can be evoked. And so on—but no device is perfect.[8]

The Actual Plan

After deciding upon the technique of the workshop, the concrete details quickly emerged, not out of whimsy or inspiration, but as informal deductions from its nature and requirements as well as from implicit principles of social science. Six representatives from each of the three African countries would be invited—six, because then there could be two T-groups of nine participants each, and during other hours of the day all the participants could form a general community for less rigorous purposes. We would meet in some neutral country, probably in Africa or the Middle East, and there, having been given the opportunity to interact in a permissive atmosphere, we would hopefully evolve one or more creative ideas having political implications for the border disputes. The issue was not to be prejudged in terms of a

Federation of the East African Horn or any other agreement. We from Yale would function as private individuals, not wedded to particular aspects of the workshop
technique but prepared to introduce any kind of arrangement that might stimulate creativity. During the
first phase, lasting about a week, the African participants would have an opportunity to learn to communicate more effectively with one another in a general
way before turning to the border disputes that would
occupy the second phase and last another week. Toward
the end of the second phase they would conceivably
discuss, perhaps even be given some instruction concerning the difficulties they would experience upon "reentry" into their own country with respect to the trans-
mission of decisions, criticisms directed at themselves
and the like.

The participants would all be academic persons of
high standing. Scholars, it was thought, would have the
psychological attributes that would make unconven-
tional change more probable. By virtue of their superior
education they would possess, it was hoped, some degree of perspective concerning the problems of the
Horn. They would not officially represent their governments and hence would not be constrained to uphold a
position previously established by the leaders of their
country. It would be extremely simple to find men with
a fluent knowledge of English, and thus the problem of
language and of any possible emotional or conventional
complications resulting from the presence of women
could be eliminated. As academic persons in Africa,
they would undoubtedly belong to the small elite and
would therefore have some or great informal influence
both within government and among their own peers.
Were a decision of significance to be reached at the

workshop, therefore, the participants would have access
to the channels along which the decisions could be communicated to men in power; but of course there could
be no guarantee that they would be willing and able to
transmit the information when they returned home or
that, if they did so, they would be heeded.

Other reasons were advanced for inviting African
scholars. It seems probable, though as yet undemon-
strated, that the two-step theory of communications is
applicable to these African societies; most Americans
are said to be influenced, not directly by the mass
media, but by informal "opinion leaders" who are attentive to the media and pass on the messages.[9] If the same
process occurs in Africa, the views of the returning participants might also have greater influence throughout
the population. Scholars who are also social scientists
might be additionally motivated to attend the workshop
if their interest in the Horn had a professional tinge; and
they might welcome the opportunity to become acquainted with the techniques of the workshop by actually participating in one. Academic persons flock to
meetings, especially if expenses are paid and travel is
involved—actually the plan called for the paying only of
expenses, without an honorarium. Although the participants, being by and large strangers from different
countries, would not constitute a "natural" group, they
would at least share certain scholarly and university
traditions and hence would possess the preliminary basis
for interacting. Finally, it was thought to be relatively
easy for academic persons from America to establish
contact with African counterparts in the three countries; all three of us had been in one or all of the
countries for research and other serious reasons, and
therefore we would perhaps be trusted as persons
working in the scholarly vineyard.

The proposal, in short, involved a preliminary attempt to determine whether a very select group of elite Africans who were not committed professionally to political power could reach some kind of creative consensus.

Pursuing the Workshop

In this section and in Appendix 1, I provide a rather full account of how the workshop was launched, not because we needed catharsis after the painful experience (in fact, we still do), and not because we wish thus to demonstrate that perseverance is one of our character traits (it definitely is), but because it seems important to record the kind of manipulations a trio of private scholars had to engage in to achieve a scholarly objective having implications for peace. To realize the plan, it was of course necessary to raise money and to invite potential participants to attend the workshop. First, major foundations in the United States were approached. While responding with some enthusiasm to the idea, they refused to lend their support because, they maintained justly, the idea was too politically tricky. They were convinced, moreover, that we could secure the cooperation neither of the governments nor of potential participants. One foundation believed that it might jeopardize its "investment" in one country by involving itself, however indirectly, in the affairs of that country's antagonist.

These objections could be met only by proving the feasibility of the plan, the first step of which demanded a gamble in money (provided generously by Yale through its president and the Concilium on International Studies) and in time through a visit to the three countries (provided reluctantly by me). The pur-

pose of the trip in the summer of 1966, then, was
clearly formulated in advance: to find six scholars or
their equivalent in each country who appeared emotionally stable and interested in the project and then
to explain the proposal to them in detail, to outline
the general and specific nature of a workshop, to indicate the kind of travail that the experience might en-
tail, to win their trust in me as a person, and in short
to persuade or induce them also to gamble some of
their own time. Since each country, of course, presented different problems, the account of this wearying,
boring, exciting, frustrating, gratifying venture is
broken down country by country and briefly given in
Appendix 1.

With some difficulty I located six highly qualified
men in each of the three countries and, usually with
even greater difficulty, persuaded them to accept an
invitation when and if we could raise the necessary
funds and find a suitable site. In Kenya and Ethiopia
the men I found held regular academic posts in the
national universities; in Somalia, which had no university, they came from the professions or held civil-
service positions having no connection with foreign
policy. They were all very busy; and indeed, they
hesitated to commit so much time to the workshop.
The university calendars vary in Africa and are also
different from Yale's; hence it was impossible to find
a time completely satisfactory to everybody. Many
features of the project, especially the unstructured
character of the workshop, were not readily grasped.
Perhaps the flavor of the conversations can best be
recaptured by translating my notes into a sequence
that, though hypothetical, reflects our responses most
accurately and also indicates the actual questions

posed by at least three and usually many more Africans.

You mean to say there will be no agenda for the conference?

No, we are not going to have an agenda, for this is not a conference. You, you Africans, you will have to decide what to talk about.

Without any help from you?

Yes, without any help, except that we shall welcome you at the beginning and tell you to run your own affairs. If you ask us, we may make a suggestion from time to time, but only with reference to procedure. For example, for a given session we might propose that our Somali friends present the Ethiopian case for the Ogaden; that is, they will play the role of Ethiopians, and we will all listen to them.

Why do that?

So that you can understand, deep inside yourselves, how your antagonists feel; you won't want to make a fool of yourself in front of us, even if you are acting.

But how can you be sure we shall talk about the disputes in the Horn?

We cannot be certain, but all of you who are being invited know why we want the workshop, and all of you are interested in the disputes and in settling them. And of course everybody is bound to realize that his colleagues in the other countries will be thinking of what they are going to say from their political standpoints; each person will therefore alert himself to his own case. Under these circumstances I think it will be impossible for you not to devote most of your time to the problem.

Should I read anything about workshops beforehand?

That is up to you; I shall send you a bibliography and literature if you wish. But perhaps the best way to find out about a workshop is to participate in one; and you may also learn something about yourself as a result of the experience.

But why invite me? I am not an expert.

That does not matter; you are a citizen of your country; you have loyal feelings which you will express.

What will all this accomplish?

That question is hard to answer. The most honest answer is: I do not know, but I have hopes. At the very least we shall discover how the technique of the workshop functions among scholars coming from countries where there is tension; we may publish a scholarly article describing the experience. In research terms we may also learn something about attitudes and how they are expressed and hence can be investigated in such a group setting. And at the very most you Africans may hit upon a new, perhaps an African solution to your territorial disputes.

And if we do?

Again I do not know, except for one thing: toward the end of the workshop it will be you, and not we outsiders, who decide what the next step should be. Perhaps you may wish to make known to your governments any new ideas you have. Perhaps you may advise us to stage another workshop with representatives of your governments as the participants. Perhaps, I sometimes tell myself late at night when I try to comfort myself for going on this wild trip which I am not enjoying, perhaps we might suggest to everybody that here is a tool—the workshop—that could be used to help resolve other international conflicts, much bigger ones.

Will the workshop be secret?

No, there is nothing secret about it—or, for that matter, about our conversation. Tell anyone you like what we are trying to do. Naturally when we come together there will be no publicity, and journalists will not be present.

Do I personally run a risk by attending?

Perhaps you do, but you must make that judgment. All I am doing is inviting you; you know the risks better than I.

Where is the money coming from for the workshop?

I wish I knew, but I promise you one thing: the money will not come from the government, the United States government. I shall try to raise it from private foundations, from private companies, from private individuals.

Why should you as an American be doing this; have you any connection with the American government, with the CIA?

The reply to these last questions could only be trite: an appeal to the tradition of increasing knowledge and also an expression of idealism.

As already indicated, no effort was made to minimize the psychic pain that can be experienced during the give and take of a T-group or at other times as a workshop sets about its task. In the course of the interview each person usually expressed his own country's viewpoint regarding the boundary—"those people cannot be trusted." The neutral silence we then tried to maintain sometimes created tension or embarrassment, but we could not deviate from our role as impartial organizers of the workshop.

During this 1966 trip, as explained in Appendix 1, clearance was obtained from the governments of

Somalia and Kenya but not from Ethiopia.

With the one exception just mentioned, then, the feasibility of the project had been demonstrated by September 1966. But this result did not help us raise the money. One glowing letter from a prominent foundation official ended by sending us on our way:

> I hate to think that I am the kind of fellow who can't respond to a good man with a bright idea in a bold and gambling spirit. There is much that I find intriguing in your idea. . . . But I find myself overwhelmed with caution and doubts. . . . I also see the step of bringing people together from the three countries as perhaps an overly delicate start. . . . I know from casual conversations with various people that there are many interesting questions here that might be explored and might have a real value in avoiding traps in negotiation or discussion. . . . It is obviously a delicate matter to do something like this on outside initiative. Even when kept in a rather academic context, it is the sort of thing which we in the foundation would approach with great caution, and in matters like this we would, I think, want the clear approval of the State Department. . . .
>
> I am sorry I can't be more constructive and positive about your proposals. When I see the funds that are chewed up in trying to pacify Kenya's North Eastern Province, and the dismaying costs to both Ethiopia and Somalia of their antipathies, I am well aware that one of the best possible forms of aid to these countries would be helping them toward peaceful mutual relations.

And so in the course of the next few months, we tried

one other way to appease timid donors: informally I discussed the project with various officials of the Department of State, most of whom played extremely important roles in helping to formulate and to carry out American foreign policy with reference to Africa. A high official suggested that he would indicate his approval—presumably on an informal level—to any foundation or person communicating with his office. Another wrote to say that "I hope very much that you are successful in finding an 'angel,' since I do think the idea has possibilities for real accomplishment."

Even when we reported the results of my trip and the attitude of the Department of State, we could obtain no financial support. The three of us underwent the humiliating experience of soliciting funds from a wide variety of foundations and private individuals. We had neither the patience nor the fortitude to grovel at all conceivable doors. With one exception—"I am sorry I cannot become more sanguine over the idea"—the project aroused what appeared to be unrestrained enthusiasm; in fact, I say with a trace of a blush, the word "brilliant" was applied to the idea. *But,* but, but: funds are low; this is not in line with our charter; this is too politically sensitive; we must wait until the reorganization is complete; we cannot invest in a high-risk, high-return proposition; and so forth.

We felt so discouraged, I now admit, that we decided to apply to the United States government for financial support. Two departments in Washington had, in fact, indicated their willingness to consider an application from us. After hesitation, vacillation, and consultation, and with no feeling of satisfaction, we submitted first an informal and then, before Christmas of 1966, a formal application to the Advance Research Projects Agency of the Department of Defense. We were of the opinion that no strings would be attached to their money, which could be administered by Yale University; and we knew from public statements that the agency had previously been interested in the general problem of conflict resolution. As indicated above, I had promised the African scholars that we would not accept money from the government, and the reason for the shift would therefore have to be thoroughly explained to them: we believed the money would be clear and free and that the workshop could function exactly as we had envisioned it would under private funding.

Individual members of the State Department's board that reviews overseas projects directly financed by the federal government—the Foreign Affairs Research Council—had on more than one occasion informally expressed their support of our project and their belief that it could win approval of the council if government funds were involved (one man was rash enough to whisper that maybe funds might even be made available from the Department of State); nevertheless, when members of the council were approached informally by the agency in January 1967, they indicated that the proposal would be turned down. Half-heartedly we tried to determine whether this ban could or should be lifted. We were painfully aware of the exposure of the CIA that occurred at the time, and we anticipated understandable suspicion among our African participants. In fact, the Department of State formed its "basic views" on our project "before" the "recent publicity on subsidies," as one official wrote us; it was feared that any kind of official sponsorship would damage our plan. Under these circumstances it was easy for us to agree with the State Department and to shift back to our original position: no government subventions for the actual workshop.*

At this point we felt not only discouraged but also paranoid. Among ourselves, consequently, we always referred to the project as the Wild Idea, so unrealistic did the chance of its ever taking place appear to us. Whenever we contemplated abandoning it, however, some friend encouraged us to carry on.

In the spring of 1967, however, prospects suddenly looked brighter. The Ethiopian government expressed its nihil obstat to the workshop as a university project, perhaps because we had received the backing of the United Nations Institute for Training and Research. In 1968 funds began to appear from two American sources, the Academy for Educational Development and the James Marshall Fund, and, with UNITAR's help, from a British trust. Foltz and Stevens, after visiting me in Dar es Salaam (where during a sabbatical I was peacefully and blissfully writing a book on the problem of time), revisited Ethiopia, Kenya, and Somalia to reactivate the interest of the African participants and to find substitutes for those who were no longer available. Through UNITAR we obtained the use of a neutral site for the workshop, a school on the island of Malta. Everything was thus all set, including

---

*These unofficial blessings of the United States government which we obtained in passing do not, for several reasons, mean that we were in effect agents of that government. The project originated with us and not in Washington or in any American embassy. We carried it out without any direction whatever from American officials; their knowledge of Fermeda has come exclusively from our published article and will now be supplemented by this book. Further, officials in at least three African countries located outside the Horn gave us off-the-record encouragement. Agreement with our government, in short, did not mean connivance; and we would have done just what we did if there had been disagreement.

an adequate supply of good, clean non-US-government money; and so the workshop was scheduled to begin in August 1968. Then the Somali Prime Minister withdrew his consent, for politically expedient reasons we could easily comprehend in the midst of our depression. The funds had to be returned, the invitations to participants had to be withdrawn. Again the project seemed absolutely hopeless.

The Wild Idea was, nevertheless, too good to drop, or so we continued to think as a result of pressures from our friends, our superegos, and our egos. The Prime Minister of Somalia had in effect asked us to postpone the project until after an election in March 1969; in fact, he won a significant victory. By the middle of June it looked as though we might obtain his consent, and we therefore adopted a strategy that involved a really final attempt to bring off the workshop *at the shortest possible notice.* Yale backstopped us financially. The same American foundations agreed again to help us "if you can get the show on the road," and Edward W. Barrett, in charge of the Academy's International Mediation Study, agreed under the same conditions to try to raise additional funds. On June 21 I once more visited Somalia. This time the Prime Minister gave us an enthusiastic "green light" (his expression). In Mogadiscio and the other two capitals the weary, weary task of rounding up potential participants for the workshop then had to be repeated and was made all the more difficult by the previous cancellations. A half-dozen men in each country who more or less satisfied our original criteria nevertheless agreed. None of them, as I have emphasized, officially represented his government.

When we had acquired the eighteen best available participants, other staggering administrative problems remained, particularly for my two colleagues in New Haven. One task was to arrange air passage for more than twenty persons departing from more than half a dozen airports on three continents so that they would arrive at one spot more or less simultaneously. As indicated, the workshop had to be held during the first two weeks of August, less than a month away. It was not easy to produce skillful, experienced, adventurous T-group trainers at such short notice. We were most fortunate, therefore, finally to obtain on a professional basis the services of the four trainers who have contributed to this volume. These men were intrigued enough by the challenge to reorganize their busy schedules at the shortest possible notice and to join in a project that at that stage had been described to them only over the telephone by persons they had never met. Finally we discovered that Malta and most of the sites we had been considering were not available in the midst of the tourist season. Others were politically unacceptable to some of the participants; one in an African country was rejected by some of the trainers because they could not spare the travel time. My panting, hard-pressed colleagues explored by telephone no less than ten possible sites in six different countries. And so I returned to Europe from Africa, headed for the South Tyrol because I know that region best, hired a car, and eventually discovered the Hotel Fermeda. Mr. Barrett energetically pursued money with which to reimburse Yale. And so we miraculously met in Rome on August 1, and the workshop began the following day and lasted until August 14, 1969.

2. The African Context and the Schedule

by Thomas A. Wickes

The Fermeda workshop was unique in some important ways, and it was not unique in many other ways. In order to understand the experience and to grasp why those of us on the project were, and remain, excited by its possibilities, it is necessary to develop the historical context in which this single event is embedded. Here and in Appendix 2 I shall outline the experience with workshops in Africa that preceded Fermeda, and I shall show in some detail how these earlier efforts presaged and provided positive encouragement for Fermeda.

In its approach the Fermeda workshop relied heavily upon a particular kind of group-oriented, experience-based learning that is referred to, among other names, as sensitivity training, the laboratory approach to learning, or sometimes, the laboratory method. The basic feature of this approach is that participants learn through analysis of, and generalizations from, their own experience and that of others with whom they interact. Laboratory participants, in different words, must first participate (interact, behave); then they are encouraged to reflect upon the meaning and impact of that behavior in relation to both themselves and others. Out of these kinds of interactions—and their concomitant feelings, bodily postures and sensations, perceptions, and so forth—grows a great deal of the learning. Through such an experience members of a workshop can learn more about themselves, the behavior of groups, and their own impact upon others. And the training can help them examine and learn more about general communications skills.

The basic configuration or unit for this kind of learning is the training group, or T-group. Participants are assigned to T-groups, usually made up as heterogeneously as possible, and meet regularly therein throughout the extent of the workshop. The group is the core learning unit.

Trainers or facilitators (trained personnel in the laboratory method) sit in the T-group to help the participants understand what is happening—to help them look more knowledgeably, analytically, and understandingly at the ways in which the group as a whole and the individual members are functioning in relation to each other. From time to time throughout a workshop, staff members present more structured experiences that help the participants better to conceptualize and understand many of their experiences in the T-group. These may range from formal lectures through movies or other audiovisual devices to the role playing of specific relevant situations or the practicing of skills that will be of use in the immediate and distant future.

There are many applied variations on this theme, too numerous to catalogue. In the managerial setting they are often referred to as management development workshops, or labs; in the educational setting, educational development labs; in a more general cross-discipline setting, human relations labs. The structured content of these workshops is, of course, designed to be relevant to the background and work of the participants at that particular workshop.

Though it was unique in several ways, Fermeda was not the first time the laboratory approach to education had been offered to Africans. It was not the first time people from several African countries had participated in laboratories or workshops. It was not the first time a multinational conference with Africans outside the African continent had contained a sensitivity training laboratory section in the program content. It was not the first time eleemosynary organizations had underwritten workshops that utilize the laboratory approach.

However, it was absolutely unique in that it was the first time these dimensions came together at one place and at one time in an attempt to analyze, define the dimensions of, and create solutions for national border problems. At Fermeda solutions to the border problems were in fact generated, and the fundamental triggering substantive issues were identified and discussed in great detail. Certain primal values and issues, almost never talked about at typical problem-solving conferences, were mentioned openly—for example, the high value of and competition for land, water, and women. These dimensions alone made Fermeda unique. But it did have forerunners in prior work done in Africa.

Early Application in West Africa

Probably the earliest systematic or semisystematic use of the laboratory approach to learning in Africa took place in West Africa starting in early 1961 under the auspices of local organizations and the Ford Foundation.[1] These were variously identified as Training Institutes or Workshops in Staff Development and Human Relations. Basically they were sensitivity-training laboratories lasting anywhere from four days (basic labs) to two weeks (advanced labs), although they differed somewhat, in a quantitative sense, from those typically seen in the United States. Relatively there were more small lectures, demonstrations, enactments, and films—general show-and-tell educative media—and relatively fewer periods devoted to absolutely unstructured open discussion time. This difference holds true for both the basic and the advanced labs and was a training strategy that evolved as a result of the experiences in earlier labs. Compared to European and American participants when dealing with agendaless or unstructured parts of a program, Africans experienced greater anxiety and nervousness. In turn, this fact prompted stringent attempts to create rules, order, and structure. There are undoubtedly many reasons for such anxieties, not the least of which may be the fact that from birth to death many Africans work very hard for their survival and have very little time for inward-turning or contemplation. Few have leisure time to learn how to live in unfilled time or with unstructured agenda. Moreover, they clearly have a base line different from that of Westerners as they begin a workshop. They may not be as well supplied through their educational systems with the fundamental sociopsychological concepts and the knowledge that allows easy interpretation, integration, and conversion of subjective experiences into everyday behavior. These general differences were noted again at Fermeda when the staff compared the behavior of the African participants to that of Americans in United States labs.

. The early series of workshops, which took place in Nigeria and Ghana in West Africa, continued on a relatively regular basis, into 1964. They included about 300 participants in roughly ten different programs. They were held in seven different locations, and one of the programs included twelve men from East Africa. The remainder came from West Africa and mostly from Nigerian and Ghanaian tribal groupings (Ashanti, Akan, Fanti, Ewe, Tiv, Ga, Hausa, Fulani, Ibo, Ibibio, Yoruba, Efik). There was a sprinkling of nonblacks among the participants, only some of whom were citizens of African nations, but they were distinctly in the minority. Five black West African women also attended different workshops. Employers were mainly government-run or government-controlled agencies, services, or corporations; some were from public corporations and small private businesses. The participants ranged in age from just under thirty to just over fifty and held responsibilities that ranged from the head of a relatively large corporation to lower-level officerships in civil-service agencies. Certainly in most ways they represented a reasonable cross-section of the general population and power structures in Nigeria and Ghana.

Participants were usually drawn from within the country where the workshop was held: Nigerians participated in the Nigerian workshops, Ghanaians in the Ghana workshops. Even within countries the workshops were often regionalized. Those presented in the Eastern Region of Nigeria almost always had participants from that region and the tribal units within the region. There were, of course, exceptions. As will be seen, it was through these exceptions and the almost accidental mixing of participants from different tribes, regional affiliation notwithstanding, that the trainers began to see a very special applied effect brought about by the workshops.

Initially these workshops were viewed as adjunctive to the general development of those in the civil-service system in the federal districts and in the other regions of Nigeria and Ghana. Participants were drawn from the various national and local governments, industry, services, and institutions of higher learning. However, most of the participants were members of the civil service because of the degree to which socialism is practiced in middle African countries. Nigeria and Ghana were both intensely engaged in developing competent civil servants to take the place of the British, who were asked to quit these countries as soon as possible. Nigeria particularly was pressing by trying to train and upgrade nationals to take the place of the expatriates. Ghana had something of a headstart and by 1961 had "Ghanaianized" most of her civil-service positions.

Crucial Problems

A number of problems arose in preparing people for the newly opening positions. One of the four key ones involved the need for a common language. There are more than 150 languages spoken in Nigeria, for example, and a common language was necessary to carry on with the administrative superstructures designed and implemented by the British. A number of West Africans who were educated primarily in Africa or in nations where English was not the principal language had difficulty in understanding each other, and verbal skills needed upgrading.

A second major problem was imparting to new or relatively untrained people the technical skills needed to administer a small civil-service unit or section: understanding and working with budgets, reading charts and graphs, understanding officials, and the like. Though a relatively straightforward task, it takes planning and the time and energy of a number of experienced people to provide the necessary information.

A third major difficulty lay in the area of supervising and/or working with others. Many Nigerians grow up within a social system that requires absolute and unquestioning obedience for the earlier part of their lives. Then almost overnight the system elevates them to peerage, where in effect they are as good as, but no better than, almost any other man around them. In short, many of the new civil-service officers experienced difficulty in learning how to deal constructively and co-operatively with those in authority in a system organized like a military hierarchy.

The largest major problem was tribalism. Though the tribes within geopolitical units of Nigeria and Ghana have many common dimensions, there are also many differences in custom and opinion. Within the tribal grouping the extended family exists as the basic unit. Among other things, that family identifies its bright children and educates them; chooses mates for its members; decides upon the distribution of family land; establishes patterns of religious practice; protects and feeds the hungry, abandoned, or ill; and punishes members who transgress the rules and rewards those who do not. All these functions produce powerful loyalties and, on the other side of the coin, do little to build trust beyond the edges of the extended family. In fact, asked in whom they place their trust, West Africans most often mentioned their senior (blood) brother first and then other members of the extended family. Occasionally they referred to someone beyond the boundaries within the tribe, but they never mentioned anyone outside the tribe.

Workshop participants, upon learning that members of a different tribe were to attend the workshop or upon learning that they were going to have to share bedrooms, dining tables, and other facilities with them, often reacted very negatively but not always openly. Sometimes they said they would leave if their room assignments could not be changed; more frequently they said very little until the end of the workshop. In the interim, at least initially, they tended to segregate themselves into their various tribal groups. Often they knew of or were acquainted with each other through other members of their own tribal group.

An Important Insight

The full impact of participants' feelings and the degree to which attitudes changed was most evident at the end of these workshops in Africa. At that point they would say to each other, and note on their written evaluation forms, such things as, "I did not think it was possible to become friends or even be on friendly terms with an [Ibo, Ibibio, Yoruba, Hausa, Fulani, Efik, and the like]." Participants frequently mentioned that they were prepared to return to their ministries and for the first time could consider hiring people from tribes other than their own. They also indicated a desire to continue the relationships they had built with other tribal members—and this happened when they were fortunate enough to live in the same city or to work near each other. Such was the case with many of the participants from the federal civil-service structure.

The seeming ability of sensitivity training to disrupt and alter long-standing, almost traditional, hatreds between groups loomed as a more and more significant aspect of the workshops. Toward the end of the series the trainers began to alter the workshop designs to focus somewhat more intensely on intertribal understanding. It seemed more and more important that people from different groups try to understand each other's socio-economic and psychological subcultures. However, this aim never became the total focus of any workshop. The emphasis continued to be on a general strengthening of human-relations skills, especially as such skills might be applied in the participants home organizational setting.

Potent though the above insight was, none of the staff members of these early African workshops talked about how this approach might specifically fit into the discussion of border problems between nations. I can recall some animated discussions, however, centering on sensitivity training as an approach to resolving the very tense conflict generated by boundary disputes. This thought was particularly applicable to Nigeria, one of the most heavily populated countries in Africa, where murders over land disputes were not uncommon.

Moreover, after returning to the United States, I made several attempts[2] to persuade Americans that the laboratory approach, appropriately staffed, applied, and funded—perhaps even set up as a part of an economic development program in an emerging nation—might significantly help to avoid such massive conflagrations as the civil war between Biafra and Nigeria. Then and later I could point to the fairly extensive use of other workshops in Africa, a detailed historical account of which can be found in Appendix 2.

These attempts to extend laboratory training into the tribal and economic arena met with little success, and it remained for Leonard Doob[3] and his colleagues from Yale to be the first to understand the possibilities of the laboratory approach and then to capitalize on this understanding in connection with border problems.

What Doob and his colleagues thought they found in the laboratory approach was an aspect of the same phenomenon that excited the trainers in the 1961-64 workshop series. It seemed a way to accelerate the pace of change. Doob saw it in connection with border problems. The 1961-64 series trainers considered it

a technique to increase the speed with which the resources within a country could be utilized in a working
system.

The Fermeda Schedule

For the sake of Fermeda's historical record, and to
guide the reader through the details of many chapters in
this book, I have compiled two charts that indicate con-
cisely just what took place in our workshop during the
first and the second week.

Editor's Note.

During the "Free Time" indicated on the charts, everyone remained in the
general vicinity of the hotel, since Bressanone, the town in the valley, was
too far away and transportation was never immediately available. Some of
the participants played cards; a few played chess or checkers, either inside
or on a veranda. Others just sat and talked or dozed in the cool sun. Small
groups wandered off onto the trails that produced new, magnificent views
of the mountains at every turn. Buckets of tea were drunk, especially by
the Muslims; little or no alcohol was consumed. Some, of course, went to
their own rooms to nap, write letters, and so forth.

During the social hour—euphemistically called 'hospitality" on the chart
—almost everyone gathered at or near the bar; conversation tended to be
lively and varied, as it did at lunch and dinner. At this time alcoholic drinks
were consumed moderately by almost everyone; and the Muslims remained
faithful to tea, while only a few of the participants drank relatively large
amounts of distilled spirits.

After the final sessions each night, many went to their rooms immediately. Others clustered at or near the bar and kept the bartenders quite busy.
But the Muslims drank tea.

For the "weekend break," starting at noon on Friday, all the African
participants except two, three of the trainers, and the executive assistant
left Fermeda for Venice on a special bus we hired; they returned on Satur-
day night. The fourth trainer went by train to Venice; the rest of us found
various ways in the South Tyrol to forget about the workshop.

Chart 1. The Fermeda Design—First Week

Time	SATURDAY	SUNDAY	MONDAY	TUESDAY	WEDNESDAY	THURSDAY	FRIDAY
8:00 – 9:00	– – – – BREAKFAST – – – –		– – – – –	– – – – –	– – – – – –	– – – – BREAKFAST – – – –	
10:00		TRAINING GROUP	General Assembly and in subgroups: game (Disarmament); theory and discussion on winning and losing as a human experience. Examine various strategies, assumptions, learnings—related to international problems.	TRAINING GROUP	TRAINING GROUP	General Assembly: the country groups and "Yales" present data from mirror exercise to each other. Discuss.	T-groups meet a discuss main issu agenda. Main ite are tribalism, ex nal pressures on tional solidarity.
11:00				General Assembly and in subgroups: theory and game—man as a human system (new-truck problem).	BREAK	BREAK	
12:00		General Assembly: theory session and exercise on cooperation/competition (assembling squares).			General Assembly: theory, effective teamwork, interpersonal competence (Johari window).	Continue with presentation and discussion.	
1:00		LUNCH	LUNCH	LUNCH	LUNCH	LUNCH	Participants prep for and leave on weekend break.
2:00 3:00		TRAINING GROUP	TRAINING GROUP	Intergroup observation in T-groups.	Development and examination of relevant data on each country/country "mirror" exercise. Meet in country groups: (1) list views of their problems with other countries and (2) prediction as to what other two countries will say about them. Yale participants do the same.	Complete presentation and discussion. Decide to form a planning commission to decide how to refine, sharpen, and clarify results. Select one man from each T-group from each country.	
4:00		Evaluation group to look back at last 24 hours of program. General Assembly subgroups.	Evaluation group.			Free time for other participants	Planning Group meets
5:00 6:00		FREE TIME	FREE TIME	FREE TIME			
7:00	HOSPITALITY AND DINNER	HOSPITALITY AND DINNER	HOSPITALITY AND DINNER	HOSPITALITY AND DINNER	HOSPITALITY AND DINNER	HOSPITALITY AND DINNER	
8:00	General Assembly. Official welcome.	TRAINING GROUP	TRAINING GROUP	TRAINING GROUP	Continue work started at 2:00 P.M.	General Assembly: planning group presents "Main Issues," group starts work on a few issues.	
9:00	What the workshop is about.						
10:00	Short lecture on process and content.						
11:00							

Chart 2. The Fermeda Design—Second Week

Time	SUNDAY	MONDAY	TUESDAY	WEDNESDAY	THURSDAY
8:00		– – BREAKFAST – –	New planning group meets at breakfast.	– – – – – – BREAKFAST – – – – – – –	
9:00	Participants return from weekend break.	T-groups individually continue the 2:00-5:00 Sunday discussion. Talk about land, women, water, and solutions to border problems.	T-groups meet. Continue to talk through their approaches/solutions.	General Assembly. Planning group shows the combined "best" plan. Violent discussion starts.	Participants pack and leave. Some finish research questionnaires. Mood/tone very somber.
10:00			Country groups meet to discuss their stand on solutions being generated.		
11:00		Both T-groups break into groups of fours for more intense discussions of issues/solutions. Meet in General Assembly to discuss possible solutions.	T-groups reconvene individually to review above step.		
12:00					
1:00	LUNCH	LUNCH	LUNCH	LUNCH	
2:00				General Assembly. Continues discussion of the "best" plan. Tempers grow short. Relationships begin to fragment, both within and across nationality and T-group lines. Deadlock.	
3:00	General Assembly: T-groups sit together and compare results of discussion they had Friday A.M. Break into T-groups to further analyze, discuss. Touch on territorial integrity, self-determination, oppression of one group by another, etc.	General Assembly. Looks at all suggestions generated to date for solving border problems.	T-groups divide into subgroups (within, not across, T-groups lines) to work on segments of solution.		
4:00				Planning group meets to try to sharpen areas of agreement/disagreement.	
5:00			T-groups reconvene individually to put together final comprehensive T-group plan for solving border problem.	General Assembly reconvenes: looks at new data; discussion. No agreement. Mood/tone somewhat dysphonic.	
6:00	FREE TIME	FREE TIME	FREE TIME	FREE TIME	
7:00	HOSPITALITY AND DINNER	HOSPITALITY AND DINNER	HOSPITALITY AND DINNER	HOSPITALITY AND DINNER	
8:00			FREE EVENING FOR SOME / New planning group meets during dinner. Decides to try to amalgamate the two T-groups plans into one grand plan. Work until task completed.		
9:00	General Assembly: theory and exercise. Brainstorming and the creative process.	T-groups meet and continue to work on problems/solutions. New planning group formed (old one dissolved) to design final steps of program.		General Assembly. Speeches are made; formal goodbyes start; very little work on project. Talk about research and ground rules for discussing this experience back home.	
10:00					
11:00					

3. Appraisal by a Somali

By Yousuf Jama Ali Duhul

My first inkling concerning the preparation for the workshop came during one of the first trips of Professor Doob to Somalia. He was pointed out to me as some sort of Yale professor who was a great expert on mass psychology. I never knew and do not know now what is meant by mass psychology. I only remember that there was a hint of something sinister in the activities of the "mass psychologist" and the nebulous suggestion of a CIA connection. Many moons later I had Professor Doob in my office talking most diffidently and self-effacingly about the workshop. His report of his activities until then were patently honest, and his frankness about the purely exploratory and tentative nature of the project was refreshing. It sounded like something that at least merited further reflection. The reflection matured into definite plans, and the time and place of the workshop were set for August 1968 in Malta.

After the project had reached the final preparatory stages—in fact, only a few weeks before the departure date—I got an apologetic letter from the organizers—(the term means in this chapter the Yale University group—namely Professors Doob, Foltz, and Stevens). The whole thing was off; one of the African governments concerned had insisted on its postponement. I was furious. Why should any government be concerned with the project? A clear understanding of my agreeing to participate was that all governments—whether African or American—were not to be involved. I certainly had no respect for my own government and had repeatedly said so in my undersized and overrude monthly, *Dalka.* I liked even less the Kenyatta government of Kenya or that of Haile Sellassie in Ethiopia. In their naked dictatorships a loudmouth like me would have been neutralized instantly. I had no doubt in my mind that the African government which had jitters at the last moment and called the whole thing off was either that of Kenya or Ethiopia. It was only later that I discovered that I was the only one with no direct or indirect government ties among the 18 African participants. My real shock came, however, when I discovered the identity of the African government that had insisted on the postponing of the workshop. It was neither Kenya nor Ethiopia, but my own. I realized then the extent to which our prejudices and preconceptions were likely to color our experience at the workshop. It was an essential realization, but unfortunately a futile one, because our prejudices and preconceptions did doom the workshop to failure.

I do not know whether any of the other country teams had a go at unifying their stands in the workshop. I very much doubt it. In the Somali team there was no formal or informal meeting of the team. In fact, I did not see any of the Somali participants between the formal announcement of the workshop and the departure from Mogadiscio. It is worthwhile to remember this fact in the light of the whispered charges of a unified Somali campaign during the workshop—an example of the undoubted surfacing of prejudices and preconceptions.

A few characteristics of the Somali team: because there is no proper university in Somalia, four of the Somali delegates were government employees, and the remaining two were private lawyers. The Somali team was the least academically qualified, boasting only one Ph.D. in a setting of universal doctorates and professor-

ships. At the same time the Somali team included Mr.
Musa Galal. I have not seen the papers of the other
contributors, but I am certain sufficient has been said
about him. But just in case there is a conspiracy of
silence among our traditional opponents (Ethiopians
and Kenyans) and their traditional backers (USA), I will
say that Musa has no Western doctorate or even high-
school leaving certificate. He nevertheless considers that
he is not less educated than other participants, a point
that was undoubtedly conceded at the workshop. He is
a walking, talking encyclopedia of Somali traditional
education. For whatever the workshop was discussing,
Musa always had an appropriate proverb, poem, or story
from Somali traditional literature. In fact, there was an
occasion at every meeting, exclusively devised and exe-
cuted by Musa, for Somali literature to be recited. It
was invariably the most entertaining part of the day and
often the most instructive. The workshop incessantly
talked about unification of the peoples of Ethiopia,
Kenya, and Somalia. Musa unified the whole workshop,
pink-faced Yankees included, by Somalizing it—and no
one objected or wanted to object.

The Problem

The Somali-Ethiopian and Somali-Kenyan disputes that
were the object of the workshop were furtively referred to as "the problem." At no time during the
whole workshop was "the problem" identified for
what it is: the problem of the Somali-inhabited parts
of Ethiopia and Kenya. I propose to present a Somali
version of the problem. The Kenyan and Ethiopian
versions will, I hope, be presented by the contributors
from these countries. It will, of course, be remembered that I have no mandate to speak for the Somali
government, or indeed for any other Somali, and that

is why my presentation will be the point of view of a Somali, and not the Somali point of view.

The genesis of the problem lies in the infamous European scramble for Africa of the last century. European-imposed boundaries haphazardly dividing tribes and peoples are familiar to any one with a nodding acquaintance of Africa. All the present African boundaries are the result of nineteenth-century and early twentieth-century European power politics and horse-trading. Africans themselves on the whole consisted more of tribes than of nations, but a territory that was "more of a geographical and ethnographical whole than any other large area in Africa"[1] was divided into five portions (hence the five-pointed star of the Somali flag). Three of these were known as British, Italian, and French Somaliland, and the remaining two were known somewhat inaccurately as, respectively, the NFD (North Frontier District) of Kenya and, even less accurately, the Haud and Ogaden of Ethiopia. The British and Italian Somalilands constitute the present Somalia; French Somaliland still constitutes the only remaining French colony in Africa; the NFD has been incorporated into Kenya; and the Somali regions of Ethiopia are, of course, still occupied by Ethiopia. The Somali-Kenyan and Somali-Ethiopian disputes result from the Somali refusal to recognize the European-drawn boundaries and from the Somali claim of the right to self-determination. The term "Somali" here includes all Somalis, whether in Somalia or in the disputed territories.

The Somali official view is that the division of the original Somali territory into five portions was one of the misfortunes of the end-of-nineteenth-century colonial scramble for Africa and should have been rectified by the mid-twentieth-century colonial scramble away

from Africa. Kenya has no right to the NFD because it
has no connection with Kenya, other than that it happened to be included in the British area as a result of the
various British-Italian colonial deals in the zone. In any
case, the people there had voted by a majority of 86 per
cent to rejoin Somalia in a referendum devised by the
British themselves and conducted by a neutral Commonwealth Commission constituted by the British. Ethiopia
has no right to the Somali territory that it occupies
because it obtained that area by being a party to the
colonial division of the Somali land, and it should leave
its portion now that the other colonialists have left
theirs.

A point that causes some confusion in the Somali
position is the five-pointed star and the consequent
charges of irredentism. The five-pointed star must be
taken in its historical context. The birth of modern
Somali nationalism has always been pan-Somali in nature, and its link to present-day Somalia is the same as
the one it has with Somali territories occupied by Ethiopia, Kenya or France. In fact, the only genuine hero of
modern Somali nationalism, Mohamed Abdulla Hassan,
belonged to Ogadenia, now in the Ethiopian-occupied
territory. Another and still more modern prominent
nationalist was Mohamoud Harbi from French Somaliland. In the present Somalia there is no difference between a Somali from the territory of Somalia and a
Somali from any of the other Somali territories. The
five-pointed star and the pan-Somali movement only
express this Somaliness.

A recent tactical shift in the Somali official position
has been to champion self-determination for the Somalis
in the territories still outside Somalia, but to play down
the reunification aspect in order to blunt the charges of

irredentism. Self-determination has been and still is a powerful instrument in the struggle for the liberation of Africa from European rule. It was thought by the Somalis that it could be an equally efficacious machine in the solving of the postliquidation effects of colonialism. Kenya and Ethiopia have retorted that self-determination is for use against whites, and that it was un-African to evoke it against fellow blacks. Most of the rulers of the forty-odd colonialism-created countries of Africa agree.

The Country Teams

The Somali team at Fermeda was a pretty cohesive group. The smallness of the educated class in Somalia and the well-known Somali homogeneity insured that. The Ethiopian team was almost equally cohesive because all its members came from the similarly small educated elite and were, moreover, present or future teachers at the Addis Ababa University. Here in Somalia we had overattacked the Amharic domination of Ethiopia. I myself have done sufficiently well in that connection in my monthly sheet, *Dalka,* to merit obscene, personal treatment by Radio Addis Ababa during the heyday of Somali-Ethiopian radio warfare in 1965.

This traditional Somali propagandistic point is not without factual basis. The Ethiopian team at the workshop was itself evidence of that. But we in Somalia underestimated one thing—the degree to which the educated class in Ethiopia as a whole is Amharized. The Ethiopian educational system is very efficient with respect to this Amharization process, as anyone could have seen from the relaxed comradeship of the Ethiopian team. The two fanatic "Ethiopians" were an Am-

harized Tigre and an Amharized Shoan. The three real
Amhara were the fairest and most open-minded in the
workshop. The lone Muslim (from a country which is
perhaps 50 per cent Muslim) was the least effective.

But perhaps there was more than mere Amharization
to explain the cohesion of the Ethiopian team. The fact
that all participants and the vast majority of the peoples
of Ethiopia belonged to racial types normally described
as Semitic-Hamitic groups may have been of some help.
It may also have been the cause of the easy rapport
between the Somali and Ethiopian teams. At personal
levels the relationship between all the participants was
pretty friendly and open. But one had the feeling that
the relationship between the Somalis and Ethiopians
was a little bit more free. Even in idle recreation, like
cards, the Somalis and Ethiopians whiled away their relaxation hours playing gin rummy. Both teams seemed
to have played quite frequently at home. But the difference between Ethiopian and Somali styles was characteristic. The Ethiopian style, which was the dominant
one in Fermeda, was much more orderly, relaxed, and
chance-dominated than the hectic Somali way.

With the Kenyan team things were somewhat different. First of all there was marked distrust and hostility
among themselves. Most of the participants had important reservations regarding their Kikuyu colleague. Some
of the participants had even suggested to me that the
Kikuyu member was there to spy on them. Their tribal
and linguistic differences hit one immediately. Even the
accents of their English varied notably. They were also
the most hostile to the American organizers and experts
in the workshop. Two of them had separately suggested
to me that the whole affair was a CIA exercise. I asked
one of them the reasons for the CIA interest. His reply

was that the participants were the intellectual elite of their respective countries (an arrogant pretension, which is not completely without some basis), the CIA wanted to probe their minds in depth and perhaps even also brainwash them. I suggested that, even if his presumptions were well-founded, we should not always be on the defensive and so assume that they could outwit us. Why could we not learn the CIA methods and machinery, or at least some of them, and so resist them more effectively at home? I obtained no convincing reply. Now I do not believe that the CIA are above doing that sort of thing, in fact, it is known that they often masquerade in academic gowns. And though I am certain that most of the organizers and experts were innocent of any such schemes, it is not impossible that the CIA had sneaked in, perhaps even wearing a black face. But I am not bothered in the least, because I really cannot believe that I could be more stupid than the CIA; or is it a case here of Somali arrogance again?

The Physical Setting

Hotel Fermeda is really in the middle of nowhere, being twenty kilometers by a steep and tortuous road from Bressanone, which itself could be described in the Italian context as being at the back of beyond. The rooms were comfortable, and the food was wholesome. The scenery, to use an expression from the "brochure" of the organizers, is spectacular.

But rooms, scenery, and food somehow were not enough. The isolation and sense of being in a quasi-prison produced muttering among many of the participants. There was a tangible undercurrent of discontent. A standard joke among the Somali team was that the expertise in psychology of some of the organizers must relate only to Whiteman's psychology. If they knew anything about Blackman's psychology, they would have realized that the monastic life imposed by them was not the most conducive to the psychological well-being of Blackmen. The above should not be taken as criticism of the physical side of the workshop. I do not know what criteria the organizers and experts had used. It may be that such isolation is essential for such a workshop. All I know is that those of us who managed to evade the monastic aspect of the arrangement did not suffer any visible undesirable side effects.

The First Week

It had been frequently remarked, during the workshop and after, that spending the whole first week in mastering the technique was too much. I suppose, if one were dealing with Englishmen or something, it might take that long to break the ice, but certainly that was not the thing for a horde of bubbling, underinhibited Africans. In fact, one of the frequent irritants was the mysticism that surrounded the "technique." We all wanted to know what the technique was. But it never emerged as a tangible thing. It will come in due course or the exercise of the moment is itself the technique—these were the standard answers. Some of the participants, particularly among the Kenyans, interpreted this attitude as insulting to their intelligence or as yet another evidence of Whiteman's disdain for African intelligence. I personally did not find any of the exercises insulting or anti–African; nor did any of the other Somalis. But I did find the pace agonizingly slow. Some allowance has to be made for the oversensitiveness of Africans who grew up in societies characterized by color prejudice in which Africans were insulted and degraded. But then one must remember that the T-group experts at Fermeda were not experts in African history.

The procedural aspects so far as they existed were excellent. The division of the workshop into two groups was certainly a good idea. But perhaps the best part about the procedural methods was that they were unstructured. As a consequence, the experts, the organizers, and the non-Somali participants had free instructions on the merits of traditional Somali procedure (Musa Galal, its champion at the workshop, would have preferred to call it African). The Ladhaye system was brought in to fill the procedural vacuum. Under it, each speaker chooses from the meeting, for the duration of his own speech, a man whom he will address. The selected addressee makes suitable attentive noises and has very primitive chairmanship powers, which, of course, vanish as soon as the speaker sits down and the next speaker addresses a new Ladhaya.

Sometimes there was need for more energetic leadership. Many of the participants found the conduct of a colorful colleague irritating. He resorted to such ruses as sitting on the floor in the middle of the circular session and forcefully taking over after each speaker by brushing aside the attempts of others to have themselves heard and by outshouting those who were not inclined to yield peacefully. I really cannot complain on that score, because the gentleman in question admitted in his final address to the workshop that he was tempted a number of times to contrive a violent collision between my head and the ashtray before him.

The Second Week

No one will take exception to the mid-conference break. The organizers had called it to get away from it all. It was only at the time of this break that any material on the "problem" had been distributed to the participants. One would have thought that there was no need for the material at all because the participants were all familiar with the problem. But that was only true of the Somali team. The Kenyan and Ethiopian teams had, of course, some idea of the essence of the problem. But none of them really knew it. The reasons for the comparative Kenyan and Ethiopian ignorance are not hard to seek.

Almost every Somali participant had been to the Ethiopian-occupied Somali area at some time during his adult life. Four of the six participants had members of their immediate families in that area at the time of the workshop. Every day tens of Somali trucks were braving the Ethiopian army by driving through Ethiopian-occupied territory on trips between the capital Mogadiscio and the second capital, Hargeisa, or between other parts of Somalia or just to go to the "rer" (the mobile households of nomads) camping deep beyond the border. Many of us had taken such truck rides, and all of us knew of someone who had suffered a tragedy because the Ethiopian soldiers found the truck. The Somali-Ethiopian de facto border is very extensive, and the people on both sides of this border are Somalis.

The knowledge of the Somali participants concerning the North Eastern Province of Kenya was not so immediate and personal; but the Somali homgeneity, the thousands of Somalis from that province in Mogadiscio, and the impact of personal contact with the ups and downs of reunification movements insured a fair comprehension of it among the Somali partici- pants.

None of the Ethiopian or Kenyan participants had anything resembling a remotely comparable personal knowledge of the problem or the disputed territories. In addition, they had no knowledge of geographically simi- lar land or people, for they themselves came from urban or farming communities. Their knowledge of the gun- carrying, camel-herding Somali nomad did not go much beyond a vague and stereotype idea of his being an arro- gant and unpleasant fellow who will cut your throat if he found you under a thornbush in a moonless night in some parts of one's own country.

A universal misconception among both the Kenyan and Ethiopian participants related to the causes of vio- lence in the Somali-inhabited parts of their present countries. They all believed that the troublemakers or the "shifta" came from the present Somalia, crossed the border, attacked the local security forces and returned to their bases in Somalia. Nothing could be farther from the truth. Almost all the major clashes occurred not anywhere near the de facto borders, but deep within the occupied territories, often hundreds of kilometers away. They invariably were between the local nomads and Ethiopian or Kenyan forces. It is probably true that Somalia has assisted the resistance groups of armed men described in Somalia as "freedom fighters" and as "shifta" in Ethiopia and Kenya. But these, too, were local Somalis and normally never crossed into the pres- ent Somalia.

I was struck by the weakness of some of the argu- ments of some of the Kenyan and Ethiopian partici- pants against self-determination for the people of the

disputed areas. A more or less general consensus among
all the participants was that, if these people are given
the right to self-determination, they will secede from
Kenya and Ethiopia and rejoin Somalia. A strong point
with some of the participants, particularly the Kenyan
participants, was that such a development would infringe the sovereignty of Kenya (or Ethiopia). The
people may be Somalis but the *land* was Kenyan (or
Ethiopian). The point that Kenya as a state and the
borders of the present Ethiopia and Somalia are all European imperialistic creations was met by the assertion
that the present Kenya and Ethiopia was what mattered,
and not the way either of them had come into being. An
Ethiopian participant had an ingenious argument for re-
fusing self-determination to Somalia. He said that, prior
to the coming of the Somalis to present Somalia and the
Somali parts of Ethiopia, the whole area was inhabited
by the Galla, who now are almost all in Ethiopia. The
Galla, being the original owners of the land, can therefore order the Somali intruders to leave. Even assuming
that the historical movements of peoples should and
could be undone, there is no evidence that the Galla
themselves would be inclined to do anything of that
sort. They constitute the biggest racial group in present
Ethiopia and yet, except for the Amharized few, have
very little say in the running of the country. If given the
choice, they would presumably ask the Ethiopian Emperor to leave their present land.

The Solutions

The two groups into which the workshop divided itself
for the purposes of intensive and detailed work arrived
at two solutions founded on two entirely differing

premises. Both groups built their respective solutions on the hope of the eventual unification of the territories of the three countries. I think it was generally accepted that such hope was likely to remain a mere hope while the current regimes remained in power. The cardinal difference between the two groups was the importance they thought should be given to the inhabitants of the "disputed territories." Group A, to which I belonged, decided that the wishes of such people were irrelevant. It was a dispute between the three countries, and solutions acceptable to them must be sought. Each of the three countries must contribute to the solution. These participants occupied themselves with the search for a "practical" formula that would be acceptable to all—i.e. a politician's solution. Their own proposal involved the creation of a buffer territory known as "the Free Zone," comprising parts or the whole of the disputed territories plus an undisputed territory coming from the present Somalia. Somalia was to contribute 30 per cent of the area of the free zone and Kenya and Ethiopia 35 per cent each. Somalia was given the right to determine the size of the zone by being the first to make a part of its present territory available for the free zone, with Kenya and Ethiopia each contributing proportionate territory. It was assumed, or course, that the land contributed by Ethiopia and Kenya would be in the undefined "disputed territories," namely the Somali areas in Ethiopia and Kenya. It would, therefore, include undetermined portions of the Somali territories in Kenya and Ethiopia and parts of Somalia. Details about what was actually to happen to the free zone if and when it came into being were intentionally left out. Self-determination was, however, expressly and categorically ruled out. Another dogma about the free zone was that the sovereignty of the respective states was to remain untouched.

Group B did not adopt the sordidly "practical" outlook of my group. They looked at the whole problem from the point of view of the people of the "disputed territory." They envisaged economic development, democratic rule, and eventual self-determination for them. They also were more honest about the measures for the unification of the three countries. It was more or less accepted by some that the current governments of Kenya, Ethiopia, and Somalia were all rotten, and that changing them would be essential for the development of a union between the peoples of the three countries. The desire for the change in government and the aspiration toward union were both palpably more honestly expressed in the B-group scheme.

The Final Fiasco

The two groups met together on the morning of August 13. The solutions arrived at by the two groups were presented to the workshop. After some discussion, it was decided that the fusion of the two solutions into one required a less cumbersome instrument than the whole workshop. A committee was empaneled to formulate final proposals for the workshop. The committee worked well into midnight. It unified the proposals that were essentially similar in one scheme and presented the remainder as alternatives.

The following morning I was personally of the opinion that the mediocre "political" solution formulated by group A, my group, would be accepted. My reasoning was that the workshop functioned by consensus. There was no machinery for majority opinion. Our solution represented the lowest common denominator and so would prevail. It had never occurred to me that we would just disperse without attempting to show something for our pains. Even little politicians issue some sort of mindless statement after a formalized meeting, even when nothing is achieved. We, on the other hand, had been telling each other that we were the intellectual elite of our parts of the world. Somehow or other we could not be less imaginative than the rulers of our respective countries whom we all heartily despised.

When the formulations of the working committee were presented the following morning to the workshop, the coolness on the part of some participants was evidenced by the critical attention to unnecessary details. It was soon clear that there had been shifts of varying magnitude in the positions of at least two of the Kenyan participants and in two of the Ethiopians. Marked undertones of hostility to Somalia and Somalis were being muttered. We were fast slipping into a state of hurling accusations at each other. Someone noted that all the Somali participants supported an Ethiopian speaker who was championing the solution of group B because, it was alleged, that solution was in the Somali interest. The organizers made valiant attempts at rescuing something. Professor Stevens was particularly full of ingenious lawyerly solutions. But neither his soothing English accent nor his usual humor were working this time. The meeting ended on a sour note.

I missed the afternoon session of the workshop. I had a severe headache and after lunch went to bed after taking a couple of aspirins. Psychologists may put whatever interpretation they like on my decision, but that was the first working session I had missed. I myself am not sure whether I would have missed it, headache or no, if I felt that we were achieving anything. But by then I had written off that particular exercise. I was, moreover, furious with some of the speakers and some of the nonspeakers as well—the speakers for attacking what they had agreed to and accepted, and the non-speakers for not defending their own work.

We assembled for the final meeting after dinner. Most of us were leaving early the following morning, and it would have required a miracle to avert failure. We did not wait for the miracle to happen. Shortly after the workshop opened, I proposed its final adjournment. The motion (and we had been talking for some time in terms of motions and formalized procedure in full workshop sessions) was opposed by some who still hoped for the miracle. I was surprised to see, at the head of the miracle seekers, my friend, Mr. Ben Kantai of Kenya. He was the most outspoken critic of all the solutions. He had more or less said openly that the solutions of both the two groups were the result of Somali trickery. My motion was quickly carried. And that was the end of the Fermeda workshop. Well, not quite, because it looks as though at least some libraries will have to come up with the cost of this book.

Conclusions

What did we learn from the experience at Fermeda? I learned that we—the African participants—had imbibed uncritically so much of Whiteman's concepts of social and political organizations that we spend all our time parroting outdated and mischievous nineteenth-century European fictions, like sovereignty, without being original or even intelligent about them. An Ethiopian friend gave an exposition on the importance of land in the

Ethiopian society and how that ingrained outlook precluded the parting with any Ethiopian land. He said that
overcrowded farmers in his home district were told to
leave their unproductive land and were offered very fer-
tile virgin land in other parts of Ethiopia. They would
entertain no such scheme because it meant leaving *their*
exhausted land, which only shows that the ordinary
Ethiopian farmer is interested in *his* land. It is a Euro-
pean-educated group that extends the original African
concept of one's land to all the political entity which is
described as "Ethiopia." An African would approach
the problem from the point of traditional occupation
and use of land, and not from the unprincipled principle
of state sovereignty.

Could the workshop have succeeded? It certainly
could have and almost did succeed in the sense of producing a paper subscribed to by all. Whether any of the
solutions in such a paper would have been accepted in
the home countries is, of course, another question. It
was conceded in the workshop that the current regimes
were most unlikely to implement any solutions arrived
at, because they had vested interests in the disputes.

Hazarding a few remarks on the utility of the T-group
concept, I think it was effective in one way. It furnished
us with some insight into the thinking of the educated
and intelligent Kenyans and Ethiopians. I had never
realized the strength of the hold of the un-African
notions of state and sovereignty among the highly educated elite of these countries. I also, of course, came to
know personally and rather intimately some of them.
That is most rewarding. The personal respect and trust
established in the workshop may eventually have direct
political consequences. The participants were men of
some standing in their countries and could conceivably

come to the top. In fact, two members of the Somali team have become ministers in the new revolutionary government of Somalia. Similar developments are not impossible in the two other countries. The personal links of comprehension could then be invaluable.

4. Appraisal by a Kenyan

by John J. Okumu

In this chapter we merely pose a few questions that have arisen from the Fermeda experiment, the details of which doubtless have been ably described in preceding chapters. The small-group technique has been used by various institutions in many countries with a fair amount of success. These experiments have, however, been carried out in various settings in individual countries, such as the United States of America, Great Britain, Japan, India, Ghana, Nigeria, Uganda, and countries of Europe and Latin America.[1] In each of them a certain structural or constitutional and philosophical framework obtains and is accepted by the majority of the population. It can, at least, be supposed that most of the inhabitants of a sovereign state share an identical system of national institutions, values, and ideals, although the social and political structure may be problematic. There, too, during the small-group experiments it may be presumed that serious and usually emotional issues such as sovereignty, territorial integrity, and so on have not arisen. These have more or less been taken for granted and attention focused upon specific problems of a college or a firm to effect its smooth operation. Although the issues may be terribly crucial for the institution involved, their overall significance and impact on the nation may be hardly noticeable.

International disputes, on the other hand, provide a more or less opposite experience. The structural or constitutional bases cannot be taken for granted, although a very broadly defined philosophical basis may be presumed to exist. The latter may be found in groups such

as the Western and Eastern blocs. This veneer of philosophical unity breaks down the moment one nation in
or outside the bloc questions the sovereignty of another
or holds claims to its territory. This act alone is capable
of transforming the relationship from one of peace to
one of war and will accordingly heighten patriotic feelings. Each nation may take an absolute stand until the
issue is solved either through negotiation and concession, where circumstances allow, or by transforming the
status quo through the defeat of one by the other.
Negotiation and concession are possible where a quid
pro quo can be effected by exchanging one territory for
another or by ceding territory for a substantial annuity
to be paid annually for a specified period.[2] All these
require special historical circumstances and considerable
good will on the part of the decision makers of the
countries involved. Also, the cost of war for both parties
must be demonstrably prohibitive to make negotiation
or concession possible. At any rate, these are the more
basic issues that involve the total survival of a people,
the nation, or the nation-state.

The disputes between Ethiopia and Somalia and
Kenya and Somalia involve the fundamental and
emotive issues of sovereignty and territorial integrity.
As shown in earlier chapters, two distinct Somalia
boundaries are involved in Somalia's "Independence
Pledge" to unite the Somalis in Ethiopia and Kenya
with those of the Somali Republic. These claims
stem from the linguistic, cultural, and historical homogeneity of the Somali. Community of culture, language, and political organization is here strengthened
by the basic economic activity of the Somali based
on animal husbandry, camels, sheep, and goats.

Background of Kenya's Stand

The present boundaries of the Horn of Africa derive from its partition by the British, the French, and the Italians. While the dispute between Somali and Ethiopia is long-standing, that with Kenya has arisen since 1961, when the two political parties of Kenya Somalis demanded the secession of the Northern Frontier District, "occupied in the east by Somalis and the west by the Boron, before Kenya became independent." Their claim was that "the act of secession be followed by a plebiscite, conducted by the non-African members of the United Nations Organisation, when all Kenyan African troops and police have been removed from the Territory."[3] The Act of Secession was to lead to "eventual merger with the Republic of Somalia." This was their irreducible minimum, the only condition which would have satisfied them. The British Government appointed a Commission of Inquiry to test the climate of opinion in the six districts that comprise the then Northern Frontier District. The findings of the Commission were not to be effected until after "an independence constitution for Kenya was brought into operation." The Commission was confronted with two basic kinds of opinion: "The Kenya Opinion which favoured remaining within Kenya, and the Somali Opinion, which favoured secession."[4] These were and still remain the dominant trends. Although the Somalis pressed for a decision before independence through a UN-supervised referendum, the British refused and preferred that the decision be made between the governments of Kenya and Somalia.[5] All attempts after that ended in a deadlock. For Kenya and Britain the issue was closed with

Kenya's independence on December 12, 1963. Once Kenya's sovereignty became a fact, any further claims to this territory by the Republic of Somalia (whose propaganda radio continued to broadcast to Somalis in the area to resist) were seen as a direct threat to Kenya's territorial integrity and an interference in her internal affairs. Giving up this territory would amount to a loss of two-thirds of Kenya's total area.

But why is it that the Kenya Somalis demanded to secede one month after the release of Mr. Jomo Kenyatta in 1961? One feeble argument for secession is that the Hamitic Moslems feared political domination by a government dominated by the Bantu (Kikuyu) and Nilotic (Luo) groups who fought for independence under the banner of the Kenya African National Union (KANU). This was the same argument on which the second party, the Kenya African Democratic Union (KADU), claimed and demanded a regional form of government (Majimbo) as a protection for minority groups in Kenya. From what is known, the demand for a Majimbo Constitution was a struggle for power rather than an earnest case for the protection of minorities.[6] This power struggle took place in Kenya between 1960 and the end of 1964 and was characterized by strong demands for regional or ethnic autonomy within Kenya. For a while the Kenya African Democratic Union, the proponent of regionalism, tried to win the support of the United Somali Association to strengthen their case for a regional constitution. However, KADU abandoned this course when it became clear that the Somalis were not seeking regional autonomy with the future Kenya nation but desired to secede. Both parties, KANU and KADU, failed to inspire the predominantly Somali constituencies in this area with Kenyan nationalism. Thus the Somali population boycotted the 1961 elections as the major parties failed to find willing Somali candidates to stand for seats. With the announcement on March 8, 1963, that Kenya had been divided into seven autonomous regions and that "the Somali-inhabited portion of the Northern Frontier District would become one of the seven regions" with a measure of autonomy, the Republic of Somalia protested against the handing over of Kenya "intact to its African government, without meeting the Somali demands for secession."[7] Thus cession of this territory of Kenya to the Republic of Somalia became unacceptable to Kenya, which became determined henceforth to preserve her territorial integrity as a cause never to be disregarded or minimized by any of her nationalists.

Kenya's stand on this issue deserves an explanation. The Somali population of the North Eastern Province is not the only ethnic group in the Republic of Kenya who can claim unity on the basis of linguistic and cultural homogeneity and of history. Take the Masai as a case in point. What is known as Masailand consists of 41,000 square miles of the eastern portion of the Rift Valley and is occupied by 191,000 Masai; 15,000 square miles of this territory are on the Kenya side and are occupied by 88,000 Masai, and the remaining 26,000 square miles are on the Tanzania side, with approximately 103,000 Masai.[8] Although there is no separate Masai nation that relates symbolically to them as the Republic of Somalia to the Somali, the Masai possess the same human qualities of nationality, common culture, language, race, and even history. As nomadic pastoralists, their cattle remain near permanent rivers during the dry season and are moved to wet-season pastures during the rainy periods. The Masai, however, differ from the Somalis in some major ways. Both Kenya and Tanzania have not interfered with the movement of Masai population across the boundary, although precautionary restrictions have been imposed whenever outbreaks of cattle diseases occur in the herds in one country.[9] As long as this goodwill continues among the leaders of the two republics, the problem of secession may not arise. Between 1960 and 1963 the Masai political leaders who supported a regional form of government demanded the restoration of their lands now occupied by the Kikuyu and European settlers. This demand was at best an electoral strategy on their part to get a fair share of the spoils of independence. They had no desire to secede.

There has also been the question of the coastal districts of the Colony and Protectorate of Kenya (as the Republic of Kenya was known before independence). Here, since 1895 these mainland possessions (the coastal districts) of the former Sultan of Zanzibar were administered by the British as an integral part of the East Africa Protectorate and its successor, the Colony and Protectorate of Kenya, "in return for an annuity." The mainland possessions included a strip of territory ten miles wide along the coast between the Tanganyika (Tanzania) boundary to the south and the islands of Lamu, Manda, and Patta to the north. The coastal strip includes the valuable ports of Mombasa and Kilindini, the rail terminus and Kenya's principal outlets. In early times Muslim Arabs formed the majority of the population of this area. They have now been outnumbered by the Miji-Kenda tribes and migrant members of up-country tribes who work mainly in the docks.

At the approach of independence the Arabs feared, rather falsely, that they would be discriminated against by an independent African government and demanded reunion of the coastal districts with Zanzibar, where they expected safety under the former Sultan. Had this demand been granted, Kenya would have lost her gateway (the port of Mombasa) to the world, and East Africa its most valuable entrepôt port. The Arab claim to autonomy for the coastal strip was in essence a quest for a bill of rights for the protection of minority groups. To resolve this fundamental question, Sir James Robertson, former Governor-General of Nigeria, was appointed to "report to the Sultan of Zanzibar and Her Majesty's Government jointly on the changes which are considered to be advisable in the 1895 Agreement relating to the Coastal Strip of Kenya, as a result of the course of constitutional development in East Africa." Right from the start the issue of autonomy for this area had to be ruled out because of Mombasa's strategic position as the chief port for Kenya, Uganda, Northern Tanzania, and the Congo. Secondly, the territory had been administered as an integral part of Kenya, and the boundaries between the colony and the Protectorate had not been administratively observed by the "government or local authorities." Thirdly, the Sultan's sovereignty over this territory was purely nominal; "the only manifestation of it on the coast of Kenya is his flag, which flies everywhere in the strip."[10] Although nebulous, the Sultan's sovereignty was definitely a serious "emotional factor" (to use Professor Ghai's expression) for the Arabs with which Kenya had to content. With goodwill and faith, and through negotiations based on the Robertson Report, satisfactory constitutional provisions were made that guaranteed freedom of worship and other juridico-religious and educational safeguards to this minority.

This second case is similar to that of the Somalis. The Moslem Arabs of the coastal strip saw themselves as

subjects of the Sultan of Zanzibar, which was developing toward nationhood. When Zanzibar finally achieved
independence in 1963, it symbolized the same thing to
Kenya Arabs as the Republic of Somalia to the Kenya
Somali. But while the Republic of Somalia claimed the
North Eastern Province of Kenya and refused to recognize Kenya's sovereignty over it, the former Sultan of
Zanzibar did not demand the restoration of the Coastal
Strip. During the 1962 Kenya Constitutional Conference in London "the representatives of the Sultan said
that they were not concerned with his abstract juridical
rights, and would be satisfied if he could be assured that
the institutions and way of life of his subjects would be
safeguarded along the lines set out in the Robertson
Report."[11] Although the Mwambao United Front, a
pressure group organized by the coastal Arabs, found it
hard to accept the former Sultan's soft line and eventual
agreement, they received no encouragement from the
Sultan, and the organization died a natural death. The
supposition here is that, had the Republic of Somalia
adopted similar procedures and an attitude of discouraging a secessionist movement among the Kenya Somalis, constitutional safeguards would have been devised
to accommodate them satisfactorily in Kenya. But this
did not happen, and the two factions moved from conference tables to the battlefield.

This background illuminates Kenya's present attitude
toward the border disputes in the Horn of Africa. First,
Kenya recognizes the remoteness of the North Eastern
Province, its general poverty, its cultural affinity with
the citizens of the Republic of Somalia, and would like
peace restored to enable development programs to be
started there. Secondly, a return to normalcy would
create conditions similar to those existing among the

Masai of Kenya and those of Tanzania who maintain a free movement of people and cattle across national boundaries. Similar conditions prevail between Kenya and Somalia with regard to the spillover of the Somalis from the Republic of Somalia into Kenya and vice versa in search of grazing and watering holes. Prescott contends that the Kenya-Somalia border dispute is further complicated by the "fact that the present geometric boundary divides tribal wet and dry season pastures."[1][2] This creates the necessity for cross-boundary movement, which is made more difficult by Somalia's persistent claim to Kenya's territory. Kenya is, therefore, very conscious of the fact that, had these two secessionist movements succeeded, it would have been reduced to a small landlocked state possessing less than one-third of its present area. There was, therefore, no better justification for the Somali to secede than the Arabs. As it is, the dispute between Kenya and Somalia is basic and relates to the very essence of nationhood. A permanent solution to this problem must be through negotiation based on recognition and acceptance of the present boundaries. Such recognition is a necessity and a preliminary to planning for peace and development.

Conflict and Its Setting

The setting out of which conflict arises determines its nature and quality. In a heterogeneous, pluralistic, and consensus-oriented society like the United States, intra- and inter-institutional conflicts occur in a context pervaded by mutually complementary values of conflict and compromise. Here conflict is seen as a process that revitalizes the established norms and values of the society. To put it another way, Sir Ernest Baker typified

such a society as one in which political compromise
involves a reconciliation of all ideas that can be accepted
by all because it bears the imprint of all. In other words,
compromise constitutes one of the main justifications
for discussion. For Edmund Burke, "All government is
founded on compromise and barter. We balance incon-
veniences; we give and take; we remit some rights, that
we may enjoy others." In his *Parliamentary Government
in England,* Harold Laski contends that a successful
representative government presupposes a nation fundamentally at one upon all major objects of governmental
activity—so fundamentally at one that the thought of
violence as an instrument of political change is incapable
of entering the minds of more than an insignificant portion of the population. In a country where the total
institutional framework of the political system evinces
such a pervasive unity of purpose and common destiny,
its population can "safely afford to bicker" without
throwing away the institutional basis of the system.[13]
In such an environment parties to a conflict would be
presumed to accept the fact that compromise may have
a greater positive meaning to them as one of the highest
political values. Where these conditions predominate,
sectoral conflicts experienced by institutions—universities, colleges, and the like—take place at a secondary
level and may not threaten the basic premises of the
political system. These sectoral conflicts contribute by
and large to the revitalization of the basic values of the
society.

In most underdeveloped countries, however, the conditions above described are either lacking or are precari-
ous. Most of the sub-Saharan African states are plural
societies governed by "profound differences of legal,
political and communal structure . . . [and] exhibit

comparable differences in legal form, substance, and modes of operations, even where the rulers hold to a doctrine of state Dicey and others summarised as The Rule of Law."[14] In other words, the central authority of the state has yet to establish itself in the country as the supreme authority capable of transforming a sectoral or ethnic ethos into national consciousness. In such countries conflict is feared for its potentially disruptive nature that threatens the authority of the state. The state becomes sensitive to all forms of conflict and cannot assume that the people accept the basic institutional framework of the political system. In such states secessionist demands pose an even greater threat to national stability than they do elsewhere.

In general, conflicts among nations differ from those within states and are characterized by a high degree of emotional and patriotic attachment to principles of territorial integrity, sovereignty, national security, and survival. Rational or not, these abstract principles tend to define conflict in absolute terms and promote the idea of the national interest, a narcissistic component of a political entity. Reduced to the defense of the self, the nation-state as a totality struggles to remain intact within its territorial confines. Claims to this territory or a part thereof become a matter for no compromise. The boundary disputes in the Horn of Africa follow this pattern in which grounds for compromise, short of recognition of existing boundaries, are reduced to naught, and the parties to the conflict resort to war.

For four years, since 1964, Kenya and Somalia were involved in a war of attrition over the North Eastern Province. When peace finally came and diplomatic relations were restored, the question as to what could be done to make the detente more permanent became the

major preoccupation of political leaders in Kenya and
Somalia. It was partly in response to this that the Fermeda workshop came to be.

The Workshop Experience

As the members of the workshop gathered in the Fermeda, one became convinced, after reflecting upon the
past history of the Horn of Africa, that no immediate or
permanent solution was possible other than persuading
each nation involved in the conflict earnestly to accept
the permanency of the present boundaries of Ethiopia,
Somalia, and Kenya. At some stage at the beginning of
the workshop one thought that time would be spent
more purposefully by up-grading ideas that would
strengthen this point and have it accepted by the claim-
ant (the Republic of Somalia) to territories of Ethiopia
and Kenya. The acceptance of this notion would be
based on the pretext that Ethiopia, Somalia, and Kenya
are what they are today mainly as a result of the colonial situation which created them as political entities.
This is essentially an argument for recognition of the
status quo that, if accepted, would involve neither gain
nor loss but would lead to a mutual recognition of the
fundamental facts of our history.

After the first meeting, which was called the General
Assembly, participants were divided into two small discussion groups. The basis of selecting people for the
groups was not explained to the delegates at all, and
there were feelings that the selection might have been
done in terms of the personalities of the individual participants. A few participants resented this simply because they wanted to volunteer for one or the other of
the groups. At the end of each day, after a series of

small meetings, the whole workshop met together to evaluate the activities and progress of each other. These were full of insights, friendly and educative. Quite apart from facilitating discussions, the T-groups were intended to effect the development of mutual friendships that cut across national boundaries. Although this was never stated with any specificity, one doubted whether T-groups were the motivating factor for this particular aspect of the experience. Friendships might have developed naturally along lines of intellectual affinities and ideological compatibility.

We also engaged in a series of games, especially after a lecture by one or the other of the trainers. Each game was supposed to reinforce the development of communication between individuals and to increase the level of mutual supplementation of shared ideas and activities. In this respect a puzzle game and some brainstorming exercises were perhaps the most successful. They enabled the people involved to develop a sense of life in the group mainly geared toward the solution of a common problem through a give-and-take process. They seemed to be successful in the T-group that followed because the participants talked very freely about them and were willing to try to engage in give-and-take in the process of discussion. For some the mastery of the workshop technique was in itself more important, as they intended to apply it to less sensitive problems in their own home countries.

However, it stands to reason that the act of going through such an exercise may take place without necessarily transforming the individual's attitude and emotional attachment to the problem at hand. This becomes even more difficult where the conflict revolves around issues such as national sovereignty and territorial integrity, which are very difficult to discuss with full detachment and objectivity. My observation is that there was no direct relationship between the development of empathy and the extent to which the delegates were able to free themselves from commitments to the policies already held by their respective governments on the issue. A few reasons may be suggested here. First, no particular individual, however critical of some of his government's actions relative to the areas under dispute, was willing to be a party to the dismemberment of his country's territory. This attitude was very prevalent among participants from Ethiopia and Kenya. Most Kenyans felt that their consciences were quite clear on this issue because President Kenyatta of Kenya had publicly asked the Somali population of the North Eastern Province to make a choice between staying in Kenya, in which case they would have to observe the rules and conditions of citizenship like anybody else, and vacating this particular territory by walking across the border into the Republic of Somalia. The principle involved is that once you allow any particular section of a sovereign state that has not achieved a measure of internal institutional consistency to secede, it becomes difficult to refuse similar privileges to other ethnic groups in the same country that may wish to declare their own autonomy. This principle was strongly held by the Kenya government at the inception of the Organization for African Unity in Addis Ababa in a series of papers presented to that body.[15] It would, therefore, be unfair of the Kenya government to concede the North Eastern Province to the Republic of Somalia and refuse the Arabs of the Coastal Strip their right to self-determination if and when they choose to demand it. The participants from Ethiopia were also of the opinion that secession of territory would involve a fair amount of the redrawing of the boundaries of most African states, a problem of greater magnitude to political entities that do not possess cultural and linguistic homogeneity.

Secondly, as long as participants from the Republic of Somalia adhered to their government's policy that the Ogaden (in Ethiopia) and the North Eastern Province (in Kenya) should become integral parts of Somalia, the Fermeda experience did not convince them to the contrary. As the workshop moved towards the end, it became clearer that the Somali delegation had become united in their espousal of this stand. At the last meeting of the General Assembly it was overtly stated that Somalia did not in fact recognize the legality of the present boundaries of the Republic of Kenya, although the two countries have restored diplomatic relations. This created a very strong reaction from the Kenya delegation: "What are the Somalis up to?" In other words, the opening up of the self during the training phase and the free and open discussions relative to the problem, its magnitude, and its costliness, together with the effort expended in the T-groups to suggest possible ways and means of achieving a lasting peace came to naught. The national boundaries hardened, and most of the delegates became the very best defenders of their own respective national interests. It thus appeared that, in the absence of any commonly shared institutions and values that could be defended cross-nationally, individual national interests and purposes became the order of procedure. Although participants came as individuals, they now found themselves in a position in which they could uphold, explain, and promote the national interests of their countries. However critical at times, they defended their countries with the greatest of candor.

But to say this is not to deny the fact that, if the workshop achieved anything of value, it was the sheer amount of facts that were produced during the free and frank discussions in the intimate T-groups. The information was of a nature that rarely comes to the surface, if ever, at regular negotiations in which public servants participate. However, the atmosphere of mutual trust and confidence which developed among the members of my own T-group went a long way towards the development of free discourse which was lively, critical, and at best creative. What cannot be said with equal confidence is the extent to which that success can be attributed to the training phase of the workshop. It is also possible to contend that the professional background of most participants could have produced the same result in the total absence of the training, which, consequently, might not have been necessary. Many of those present were exposed to the idea of sensitivity training for the very first time and would have liked to have read some selected pieces dealing with the history of the technique. They were utterly disappointed and felt all along that they did not want to be used as guinea pigs. Therefore, rather than be taken advantage of, some of them decided to "sit in and observe" the process, which they did with utmost effectiveness, as their later observations suggested. The more attentive of them summarized the whole experience by saying, "If this is what social science is about, I am glad I am not a social scientist."

One of the main problems at the beginning of some small-group discussions was how to get started. Members of the group gathered together and sat there looking at each other until someone started them off. The common starting pattern always came in question form, like "What shall we discuss today?" This was more frequent during the training period and almost completely dis-appeared as the workshop plunged into consideration of the substantive material directly related to the border disputes. There was an atmosphere of restraint in the small group during the training period that might have been caused by the insistent intervention of the one or the other of the trainers who were trying, dutifully, to give every member of the group a chance to talk. As it happened, one or two members of the group were not particularly adept at verbalizing their reactions to the ideas and suggestions put forward by their colleagues. Their contribution should not be negatively categorized, because they talked quite freely about the happenings in the small-group discussions after adjournment and were very critical of several aspects of the whole atmosphere and the nature of procedure.

At times, perhaps for lack of something to say or in groping for a more worthy subject to discuss during the first few days following the beginning of the workshop, one of the T-groups ventured into more general topics, such as conflict or the role of the Organisation for African Unity as an instrument for the settlement of disputes. Some members of the workshop had more information relative to either topic than others and tended to dominate the discussion. This was falsely interpreted by the trainers as lack of interest on the part of those who remained silent but who were nevertheless receiving and thinking through vital information. However, the desire of the group to find some general topic related to the disputes was in fact an attempt to prepare more fully for the substantive discussions that were expected to come after the first week of training. This development may also be explained as a form of escape from the trainers, whose motives were not fully under-

stood although we had been assured that they were present for purely technical and professional reasons.

The move to more general areas of discussion was intended to effect a comprehensive perception and understanding of the nature and types of conflict. The border
disputes would have been classified as highly disruptive
conflicts characteristic of the international environment.
This effort did not go very far and was abandoned
rather abruptly as a digression. The attempt should be
seen, however, as having come from a desire to lay some
theoretical background for the discussion of historical
facts.

The proponents of this approach decried its abandon-
ment by the majority of the group, who argued that the
whole tone of the discussion was becoming too theoretical and not coming to grips with the real world. To this
majority the real world was that of solutions suggested
at random after the fashion of the brainstorming exercise. Their assumption was that the nature of the disputes was understood and should be taken for granted.
This was a wrong assumption, as the substantive discussions revealed later on. Something more basic needed to
be done: in a situation as complicated as the border
disputes in the Horn of Africa, solutions qua solutions
might carry very little weight in the absence of a profound commitment to some broadly based principle or
principles. Commitment to a set of principles might, as
it often does, succeed in freeing the individual from
uncritical attachment to his country's national interest
and enable him to approach a crisis with an open mind.
That would have moved us a stage farther than our
national leaders have gone on this issue.

Participants from Kenya had suspected long before
the workshop began that the Somali delegation would

seize every opportunity to justify their standard claims on ethnic grounds. The Kenya group also assumed that the Ethiopian participants and we would see eye to eye on most issues. In short, we were instinctively prepared to defend Kenya's position if need be. We took this for granted, and it did not strike us as odd, at least from the point of view of the fact that we could differ in our individual interpretation of the position the Republic of Kenya has so far taken. At any rate, participants argued subtly but never gave way from a commitment to their country's goals. This was very evident at the last meeting of the General Assembly, when a member of the Kenya group argued persuasively by quoting from Churchill that he would never be a party to the dismemberment of his own country. Thus every aspect of the Fermeda workshop tended to confirm the supposition that intellectuals as creators and circulators of culture within a historical context in time are the most convincing promoters and defenders of that configuration of interactions that constitutes the national interest. Although they claim to belong to an international community of professional scholars, they are first and foremost members of particular national representations, which constitute their historical foundations. Small wonder, then, that the national group remained the most viable unit of interaction throughout the workshop experience.

This national group was one of the basic factors that influenced the extent to which participants were free to deviate from their country's national purpose. The deliberations, therefore, tended to be tough, emotional, and sharp and were often characterized by sophisticated and even open bargaining between participants in order to effect a particular solution. This give and take was carried on with utmost seriousness. Once our T-group recognized this as the modus operandi, reciprocal concessions became the rule. As a result, the final points arrived at were very acceptable to the whole group, and every member developed a fair amount of attachment to its final product.

One of the most difficult issues was the idea that the principle of self-determination, to be exercised only under certain conditions as a theoretical right of every man, should form the basis of a lasting peace in the Horn of Africa. The subtlety of this point did not become clear to all members of the T-group: its essence was that none of the parties to the conflict would evidence any visible gains. The economic and political preconditions for the exercise of this right by the inhabitants of the disputed areas would demand exacting sacrifices from Ethiopia, Somalia, and Kenya. Firstly, the disputed areas would have to be defined anew or redemarcated in such a way that Ethiopia, Somalia, and Kenya would be bound to give up some of their present territories to be included in the newly defined area. The Somali participants objected passionately to this suggestion, on the ground that the presently contested areas do not include any portion of the present boundary of Somalia and that only Ethiopia and Kenya should cede territory. On the other hand, Ethiopia and Kenya insisted that any compromise that does not involve a fair amount of sacrifice by all the three would be meaningless. And although our T-group was able to go over the hump on this issue, the other T-group had completely avoided any discussion of the principle of self-determination and was very unwilling to commit itself when this issue finally came before the General Assembly. Our T-group felt that demilitarization, neutralization, joint economic development and administration of the disputed areas were to be based upon acceptance of this basic principle.

Some of the preconditions were very simple and ranged from the parties' being asked to accept a certain amount of discipline by ceasing to incite the populations of the disputed areas through radio broadcasts to the kind of authority to be utilized in the administration of the neutralized areas. However, many questions of detail connected with demilitarization, neutralization, joint economic development projects, and so on were really not thoroughly discussed. Although these details were not considered, it is nevertheless a fact that our T-group did not avoid any subject, however sensitive. This attitude and open-mindedness enabled us to probe many more controversial issues than our colleagues in the other T-group. In other words, we were more prepared for the last meeting of the General Assembly than our friends, and it was noticeable that the initial polarization at that last meeting arose from among the members of the T-group that had avoided potent questions such as sovereignty and the principle of self-determination.

Other commonly agreed-upon solutions were obviously less controversial and are capable of being implemented now that diplomatic relations exist between some of the countries involved. One of these was to increase the traffic of cultural and general educational exchange for purposes of sharing certain training facilities like the Faculty of Veterinary Science at the University College, Nairobi, as well as opening doors to Ethiopians and Somalis alike to benefit from institutions like the Egerton College at Njoro, Kenya, which trains agricultural staff. The establishment of the Uni-

versity of Somalia would make possible exchange of
staff and students at the university level. Properly managed, these programs may in the long run create a firmer
basis for bilateral and multilateral cooperation in a
larger Eastern Africa. Joining the East African Community by Ethiopia and Somalia was also suggested as a
standard solution that could bring the economies of the
countries at conflict closer together through the sharing
of common services and the eventual creation of a common market to facilitate movement of labor and other
commodities across national boundaries.

Lastly, there was the question of external component,
the relations between the parties to the dispute and the
industrialized countries. This is always a very unreliable
issue because it is difficult to determine the extent to
which it is a major factor in the border disputes in Eastern Africa. But because it kept recurring during the discussions, it should be mentioned in relation to an arms
build-up in Ethiopia, Somalia, and Kenya. When the
Kenya group met together to consider their general
complaint against Somalia, they noted without exception that the external component was certainly a major
factor in the relation between Kenya and Somalia regarding the North Eastern Province. They concurred on
the point that, if the Russians had given no arms to
Somalia, the fighting would not have intensified. The
Kenyans, therefore, stressed the significance of this
point by stating that "Somalia was being looked at by
Russia as a stepping stone to Eastern Africa and therefore being substantially armed." Our Somali colleagues
did not expect us to say this about their country and
became very sensitive. Our main intention here was to
launch a point of self-criticism that we conceded applied
equally to us in our relation with Britain, and the So-

malis were perfectly free to deliver a countercharge. However, the overall effect of the statement strained our relationship with our Somali brethren for a few days. The issue of general foreign aid also came up in a different light. There was a general consensus that Ethiopia, Somalia, and Kenya should not make arms deals with foreign countries for purposes of war: it is an expensive exercise, which their economies cannot afford at this time. What was not considered with equal amount of care is the fact that such arms deals are usually intended for purposes of internal security within each nation-state.

Conclusions

On reflection, the workshop experience provided a fairly flexible atmosphere for discussion among individuals, many of whom would not have had an opportunity of meeting in the near future. Most participants admitted having gained some insights into the difficulties facing their neighbors, and they developed a tendency to sympathize with them. This new realization, however, seemed to have failed to create a common conception regarding the best solutions to the disputes. By and large many Kenyans and Ethiopians reinforced their notion that the Republic of Somalia found the disputes advantageous in the management of her internal contradictions.

The main question that arises from all this is: what is to be done with the sheer wealth of knowledge and information gained during the two weeks of discussion? The majority of participants are not public servants and play little or no part at all in the formulation of public policy in their respective countries. There is, therefore, the possibility that this information may disappear without being shared with others. A way might be found for a revitalizing exercise that could occur through follow-up workshops to be designed with a narrower focus. For example, each follow-up workshop would concentrate on only one disputed area, for example the Kenya-Somalia one, and thoroughly exhaust all the possibilities and historical points peculiar to it. The next follow-up could then take up the Ethiopia-Somalia border dispute and go through the same exercise. My preference for this approach derives from the rather dispersed and often diffused discussions in the Fermeda workshop, with the result that neither dispute was treated with a maximum amount of thoroughness.

From another angle, the workshop was too loosely put together and too permissive. A little effort to guide the general atmosphere right from the start might be tried in future planning. Some measure of regimentation might have made the training phase more meaningful and serious as a learning process. This change would involve a slight departure from the basic unstructured principle upon which sensitivity training is based. Alternatively, the same effect might be effected in the selection of potential participants.

The small-group approach seemed a fairly effective technique for arriving at consensus. It was noticeable that individual members of one T-group were "completely" accepted, as were their ideas, which were freely received and thought through in an atmosphere of mutual "trust" and "confidence." This fact may have been responsible for the greater output in that group. The nature of bargaining that took place there was in direct contrast to the General Assembly, which became an anticlimax: many individuals spoke up mostly for pur-

poses of exhibition, a characteristic of public negotiations and parliamentary procedures. Perhaps for this and
other covert reasons the consensual basis of group
action exhibited in the small T-groups was totally lacking. The General Assembly thus fell short of the expectation that it would be an integral part of a process
generating better communication and understanding of
vital questions.

Nevertheless, the T-group process had a persistent air
of unreality about it. Although participants claimed to
have achieved a sense of mutual "trust" and "confidence," they tended to express doubts as to whether the
workshop succeeded in providing a sufficient framework
with which sensitive questions of territorial integrity
and sovereignty could be managed. These issues are the
real problem around which the border disputes revolve
and which require a solution if there is to be a permanent peace. They have special significance to the states
involved, as they would to any independent political
entity. The phenomenon of the territorial state has
more immediate meaning for recently created states
than for older ones. A supreme power over territory is
not only a political fact but also the very essence of the
states' being. It is the symbol of a new consciousness,
which must be expressed as being that "particular aspect
of the supreme authority of the individual state which
consists in the exclusion of the authority of any other
state."[16] It is the basis of national identification. It is
upon these principles that nations claim and possess the
right to make and execute any laws without external
interference. The violation or rejection of the right by
another state constitutes interference.

Because of its nature and meaning, territoriality poses
the greatest problem to the settlement of these bound-

ary disputes. Kenya's contention is that Somalia's claim
to the North Eastern Province constitutes a violation of
her rights and insists further that cultural and linguistic
grounds are not a basis for claiming the territory, since
no evidence is available to show that there has been any
form of discrimination against the Somali population
resident in Kenya. Besides, the government of Kenya
has had no desire to impose a new form of culture on
her Somali population. Kenya's position on this issue is,
therefore, based on the premise that a solution to the
border question must depend upon recognition by the
Republic of Somalia of Kenya's sovereign right over the
North Eastern Province in the same way that Kenya
recognizes the territorial integrity of Somalia as presently defined. Upon this reciprocal negotiations for a permanent peace would then be placed on firmer foundations.

What, then, is to be done to bring this about? One
school of thought has contended that negotiating techniques have remained conventional in the midst of a
change and have therefore rendered themselves less
functional in a world complicated by the cold war. This
school now supports the quest for new techniques emphasizing internationalism rather than nationalism.
Nationalism is seen as a major cause of wars and other
human dilemmas and hence is conceived as a negative
factor in the process of human development in this century. The school then proceeds to argue for a world
government based on transcendental yearnings for human survival in an era complicated by nuclear weapons.
But, as far as we are concerned here, this goal is desirable, yet insufficient conditions have been formulated for
its realization. It is not enough to say that nationalism
possesses negative propensities for war without ana-

lyzing the conditions that lead to a particular war or conflict. For all practical purposes the force behind nationalism is directly related to the exercise of principles of sovereignty and territoriality insofar as they relate to and affect national security. To effect a peaceful world for man, optimum conditions of natural security must be prevalent as a basic condition. To bring this about, the primacy of the concept of nation or nation-state must be accepted, and not dismissed, before a major forward movement is started in the direction of internationalism.

A community of nations is founded on the basic acceptance of the principle of sovereignty. It is therefore important that in connection with the disputes in the Horn of Africa every attempt should be made to accept sovereignty as the irreducible minimum in all forms of negotiations, whatever their nature. With this done, the question of territorial claims would be reduced, and major efforts would then be expended on the development of areas under dispute to achieve maximum satisfaction for the inhabitants involved. The dispute between Kenya and Somalia over the North Eastern Province of Kenya has so far led to greater impoverishment of the Somali people of Kenya because war conditions could not coexist with the planned economic development of the area. The continuation of war or potential conflict results in uncalled-for advantages to the other regions of Kenya and in utter disadvantages for the North Eastern Province. It further perpetuates and worsens the process of uneven development of the country experienced during colonial rule.

Sovereignty is the question the Fermeda workshop should have dealt with as a matter of primary importance. Had we tried to up-grade the idea of mutual and reciprocal acceptance of sovereignty and territorial integrity of the nations concerned within the present territorial definitions, a major breakthrough would have been made. It is on this basis that the actual significance of the various exercises connected with the T-group technique can be questioned. We refer here to the puzzle game as a case in point. This game presupposed the existence of mutually reinforcing values among participants in whom or in whose societies these values in fact may only have rudimentary force. But it is possible to see the significance of this game in situations where an alternative arrangement is capable of diverting or reducing conflict. For example, if one person wants the window opened and another wants it shut, a compromise may be brought about by opening the door instead. But this kind of disagreement is not as basic as conflict over sovereignty, which takes absolute forms. In such conflicts, opening the door may amount to much more than a particular country is willing to put up with and also depends upon who is responsible for the suggestion. Although the games and the whole context of the T-group technique is meant to maximize the significant transformation of attitudes of individuals, it is quite another question to consider the extent to which this procedure becomes a social force, particularly in conflicts involving territorial claims. The Fermeda workshop was the first known attempt to experiment with the technique in conflicts among nations, and it may be too early to judge its capabilities from only one experience. For this reason the questions we have posed should be regarded only as preliminary observations and hence subject to correction.

5. Appraisal by an Ethiopian

by Andreas Eshete

In the summer of 1969 I agreed to attend a meeting designed to discuss the dispute between the Republic of Somalia and her two neighbors, Ethiopia and Kenya. My interest in the meeting stemmed from the belief that the general problem for discussion is of central importance to my own country and Africa as a whole. The importance of the question of national minorities and related ethnic religions and regional conflicts is twofold: first, ethnic and religious domination of many African peoples is a manifest reality; second, at least in the early stages, many struggles against social and political oppression in Africa are waged as an aspect of resisting ethnic and religious inequality. In short, this pressing problem is genuine in its own right, and its repercussions for the fate of social and political movements can be hardly ignored. Although the question of ethnic and religious oppression has frequently come to the forefront as the object of bloody conflicts in many parts of the continent, it has rarely been the object of critical reflection.

There was reason, although by no means conclusive, to expect that the proposed discussion would stimulate new thoughts departing from the rather stale exchanges at state conferences and bargaining tables. The main reason for this reserved optimism was the fact that the discussants were to consist largely of academicians and a few civil servants from the countries in question. Academicians and the wider group of educated Africans commonly dubbed "intellectuals" do not usually form a homogeneous group. Academicians, like the urban lumpenproletariat to whom they bear strong structural resemblances, occupy a peripheral position in the social order, which accounts for much of the diversity in their composition. They come from varied social classes. They hold no direct vested interests in the state. They do not readily subscribe to the prevalent outlook of their societies. The heterogeneous constitution of this group and its peripheral stance with respect to more predominant sectors of the population does not thereby mean that it is a disinterested spectator. The occasions in history have been too frequent when intellectuals and their impoverished counterpart, the lumpenproletariat, have been passionate partisans of the forces of progress or the quite different forces of reaction. The intellectuals' special status within the social order only means that their views cannot be easily anticipated. The warranted expectation from this group is, therefore, a presumption against uniformity. Further, the arrangement for the discussion between these men at Fermeda was intended to be conducive to critical reflection. The talks were to be held in an isolated location in Europe, where the participants would be compelled to dwell on the fundamentals through the use of a method promoting intensive encounters. Thus the discussants and the conditions for discussion promised a more than superficial dialogue on the conflict between the three countries.

This brief essay is intended as a report on these meetings. It is not an explanation or a theory about the dispute. References are made to the nature of the conflict only insofar as they throw light on why the discussions took the direction that they did. First, I shall describe the experiment to suggest that my expectations were disappointed. My assessment of the meeting is that it was a failure. Second, I wish to draw the unexciting conclusion that, as a result of the nature of the problem at hand, it is unlikely that a discussion of this sort can succeed. Finally, I shall make a few brisk remarks of an exploratory nature to indicate where one might look in search of a resolution to these problems.

The Workshop

The technique employed in these meetings is what is called the T-group method. The guiding thought of the method is that dialogue can be fruitfully conducted if the interlocutors develop self-awareness and awareness of others. The nature of the awareness is given a heavily psychological interpretation. That is to say, the objects of awareness range from the manners of individuals to those things they prize with passion. Such knowledge can supposedly facilitate clearer appreciation of a person's position on questions. One can know what to place weight on, when something is said. Further, the interchange can be honest and straightforward, since with everything now open to view, the need to conceal becomes unnecessary. The result, if successful, would be a closely working group engaged in serious investigation. Since the findings of such an investigation would not be abstract solutions to an inquiry but the overcoming of a difficulty felt by concerned persons, there is also a belief that the participants will attempt to actualize their conclusions in practice. From this rough sketch of the technique as it was recounted to us, it is clear that these are lofty ideals in any context.

It was the intention of the trainers that the group immediately proceed to an employment of the method at the first gathering. This was resisted by the group, which called for an explanation of the method, and this the technicians were, in turn, reluctant to furnish. After some debate there was a not altogether enthusiastic decision to go ahead with the experiment. The whole group was divided into two subgroups (the T-groups) within which all three nationalities were represented. Throughout the period the discussions within the smaller groups were supplemented by general meetings. In the first week the groups were urged to focus on the purported aims of the technique by avoiding the purpose of the meeting and by concentrating instead on other analogous disputes. The second week was devoted to the border dispute itself.

The proceedings of these meetings cannot be easily described in any detail, for an adequate description would perhaps require a verbatim account. Instead I shall attempt to do what a verbatim account cannot accomplish; namely, an evaluative assessment of the efforts of the group. A broad assessment runs the risk of ignoring or glossing over important individual viewpoints, of which there were some with major differences. To capture these would require something of a literary talent that I do not possess. A more modest alternative would be to point out exceptions to the general trend as I go along. But to avoid the tedium of repeated guarded talk, I shall speak of the group as a whole and ignore the quite divergent opinions that a number of individuals continually urged against it.

The discussions in the T-groups during the first week were without important consequence. Since the aim of these earlier discussions was to advance the self-awareness of the group by staying clear of the important conflict, much time was spent on finding subjects of common interest. When topics were finally found, it was difficult to analyze them profitably: there was little time to formulate the problems in such a way that they would lend themselves to engaging discourse. Broad and ill-defined issues of topical interest encouraged platitudinous utterances that were singularly uninformative. Very little could be known, for example, of the ideological orientations of the participants. In their choice of topics and the views they advanced, the speakers were reluctant to explain their ideological stances. An indication of this would have made for clarity when we came to deliberate upon the border dispute. The trainers, who gave a highly psychological interpretation of self-knowledge, regarded ideology as something that was not of deep concern and hence distracted attention away from the real intentions of individuals. Given these limitations, the activities of the participants can only be described as acquiescence or mere playing along with the activity of the group and the method under which it was to be guided. In other words, the principles of the method, if any, did not win acceptance as ways of securing insight into the activities of members of the group. Both the arrangement of the discussion and the manner in which the participants entered the arrangement precluded any serious engagement. Since just such engagement was the avowed goal of the technique of deliberation, the aims of the method were unrealized.

Once we turned to a consideration of the actual border dispute, the more interesting exchanges that followed were marked by a pervasive lack of principles. There was little pretense of pursuing self-awareness and awareness of the group that characterized the earlier talks. Consequently the acquiescence or playing along with the techniques of discussion was abandoned. In these later sessions there was no lack of strong views; what was wanting instead was a coherence in the views themselves, a coherence which can only be attained through adherence to principles. To cite an example, there was a proposal in one group that the right to self-determination of the Somali people within Ethiopia and Kenya be recognized. Many individuals vacillated from acceptance to rejection of the recognition of this right. There is, of course, nothing surprising about this, since the nature of the right—who possesses it and under what circumstances it is to be exercised—are vexing questions requiring much empirical inquiry. What was surprising about these vacillations, however, was that they were largely based on the territorial concessions that were taken to be the consequence of the recognition of the principle of self-determination. Even among the Somalis, whose government has called for the exercise of self-determination by the Somali peoples in Ethiopia and Kenya, the main criterion for their acceptance of the principle turned out to be territorial. If territorial gains or losses are to be the sole basis for recognizing or rejecting the principle of self-determination, then the principle has been rejected outright.

As the meeting was approaching its end, it became clearer that a majority of the participants were intent on promoting the interests of their respective governments. The mask of analyzing the problems of minority peoples was quickly discarded, and the role of negotiators for sovereign states was readily assumed. The Africans were encouraged in their role as negotiators by the rest, who interjected a false note of urgency on the necessity of reaching a settlement. There was little of interest communicated at this juncture. The usual platitudes of regional cooperation, buffer zones, federalism, and combinations of these were forwarded. The orthodox arguments supporting the claims of each party were rehearsed and the principle of territorial sovereignty was quickly reaffirmed. What was of interest was not what was said on behalf of these suggestions, but the fact that they were said at all. Territorial sovereignty, upheld by a majority of the Ethiopian and Kenyan group, is just the point that the Somali want to question. Thus, the assertion of territorial sovereignty is an especially otiose gesture toward discussion between the parties. The affirmation of territorial sovereignty simply signified the acceptance of the official government positions and the rejection of the very idea of discussion, and indeed even of negotiation. Once it became clear that the claim to territorial sovereignty, under the circumstances, amounted to a decision to stop all discussion, the deliberations came to a halt. These discussions closed at a point where discussions of these questions usually commence. There could not have been a more radical departure from critical reflection than in the final resort to a dogmatic assertion of official positions.

The failure of these meetings does not, of course, mean the failure of the method adopted for conducting them. Indeed, the disappointing outcome might very well signal the success of the technique. The method of discussion calls for independent evaluation.

The leading idea of the technique employed in these talks is to draw attention to the importance of self-awareness and awareness of others for genuine dialogue. There is nothing novel about this idea. From the seminal writings of the Socratic dialogues to the Chinese Cultural Revolution, self-knowledge has been assigned an important place in the relations among men. These great historical occasions of a deliberate turn to self-knowledge are distinguished from the technique of the conference by the presence of two different, though related, elements in the latter: first, the T-group method gives a psychological interpretation of self-knowledge; second, the method makes claims to being scientific, in the sense of being susceptible to empirical testing.

It is difficult to find justification for the reduction of self-knowledge, even in its common-sensical everyday sense, to the psychological. It is not true that these psychological elements are those things in which men have an overriding interest. Men do sacrifice what they find psychologically comforting and desirable for ethical and ideological ideals. And the grounds for the sacrifice cannot in turn be psychological. Indeed, we are prepared to acknowledge a person's ethical and ideological commitments whether these psychological phenomena are present or not. I am not saying that psychological factors do not have any bearing on men's actions at all; I am only saying that they are not the only or even the necessary factors, as the method suggests. And even if there is harmony on the psychological level—whatever that means—there is no reason to think that this spells agreement in beliefs and conceptual frameworks. And should there be agreement on beliefs and conceptual frameworks, there is no reason to think that the agreement rests on what is right or true. In light of this, the method's undue emphasis on the psychological suggests that it is intended for a limited domain. There are certain spheres of human affairs where there is agreement regarding interests, and the only questions concern the realization and distribution of these interests. For example, in bureaucratic situations, whether they be in government or business, there are rules defining the goals of the enterprise as well as the manner in which these goals are to be attained. Although perhaps vague, there are qualifications that have to be met by those holding these offices. In these circumstances, where many perplexing questions have been defined as outside the scope of the offices, harmony in the personal relations of the bureaucrats can possibly increase the efficiency of organization. Similarly, where trade unions have become machineries bargaining for a greater share of the same, psychological harmony can facilitate the settlement of disputes on the distribution of agreed-upon interests. In the dispute between the three countries, the psychological could not feature prominently, since what is at stake is not simply the distribution of interests. What is being challenged is the very legitimacy of the interests of the parties under dispute.

The psychological reduction may be guided by another goal. There is a temptation to think that, if we look inward, somehow we will grasp the roots of many complicated problems. But there is no reason to think that the complications would not arise within. It is also a belief that has won wide acceptance in contemporary social science that dealing with a few simple and isolated elements somehow yields certain results. There is no ground at all for this belief. Indeed, it might be that the particular and indeterminate is just as baffling as the wider phenomena of which it is a part. Even if the trainers and the organizers were aware of the problematic and limited claims of the technique, as perhaps they are, recognition of these facts does not alleviate the difficulties of putting the method into practice. In the actual situation, when substantive claims are advanced, it is not clear whether the object of attention is the speaker's motives and intentions or the contents of his views. In the use of the technique it is difficult to avoid this air of ambiguity, which can only be confusing and, on occasion, even embarrassing. In short, the psychological reduction of self-awareness under the technique has few theoretical and practical merits to recommend it.

A second distinctive feature of the method used in these talks has to do with its claim to testability. To decide if this claim is justified, let us suppose that the discussion were successful and resulted in illuminating insights into the nature of the dispute. Could we then have said that the method proved successful? No clear answer is forthcoming, since the success of the talks could be attributed to any of a wide variety of factors. In other words, there are no criteria in terms of which the success of this application of the technique can be determined. And if the method cannot succeed it cannot fail either. Thus, my criticism of the method employed in these talks is not that it failed. The method is open to a more basic criticism: even if it delivered the best results, there was no unambiguous way to ascertain that it did have such a desirable consequence.

To summarize: the discussion in these meetings did not give rise to many thoughts that were not commonplace and sheer official dogma. No independent verdict can be reached with respect to the mode of discussion, since it does not admit of any straightforward evaluation. This is not to say, of course, that this or another form of negotiation, under different circumstances, would not come up with lasting solutions to the problem of the Somali minority peoples within Ethiopia and Kenya. It is to a consideration of this that I shall now turn.

The Dispute

When the problem is posed as a "border dispute," there is a danger of being misled by the spatial designation into thinking that what is in question is a difficulty unrelated to the internal social and political structure, and as such it is primarily a conflict between states. Accordingly, the solution that readily offers itself is that of negotiation and, failing this, settlement through war. This diagnosis and this prescription are not peculiar to this problem. In the far more heated and more extensively discussed Arab-Israeli conflict, it is not often that mention is made of the social and political aspirations of the Palestinian people. What I want to suggest is that the problem with the Somali minority people—as well as other ethnic, religious, and regional conflicts—is to be located primarily in the internal social and political structure of the African states. Accordingly, a solution to these problems through negotiation between states can only be arbitrary and short-lived.

It is an often repeated truth that colonialism created arbitrary divisions between peoples in constituting social, political, and administrative units designed to facilitate the exploits of imperialism in African territories. What is seldom mentioned but is just as significant a feature of the brutal westernizing or modernizing mission of imperialism is the arbitrary character of the treatment of African peoples within these unities. In the constitution of the unities under the rule of imperialism, the establishment of tribal groups out of more complex and sometimes simpler forms of social organization was a conscious colonial policy. The result was the formation of tribal entities where none had existed and the strengthening of ethnic divisions where they had obtained. An example of this effort to create tribal groups in the midst of more complex and differentiated forms of social organization is the British colonial measure of appointing tribal chiefs over the Kikuyu people. I am not suggesting, of course, that the establishment of mutually exclusive ethnic entities took a simple and straightforward line of development, as is suggested by this colonial administrative fiat in Kenya. There were other, more protracted, and indirect ways in which the same result was secured. The present day cohesiveness of the Kikuyu, for example, is to be attributed in part to their dispossession by the British which led to collective struggles through which the Kikuyu became an increasingly united people. The Unity Oaths are one mark of the Kikuyu's growing cohesion through struggle. The creation of these rigid ethnic divisions under colonialism was not just an administrative convenience. In many cases it was guided by important economic interests. For example, in the case of Kenya, by forcing the Kikuyu into limited and poor areas, the colonial settlers created an inexpensive labor force to work on their extensive and rich holdings. But perhaps the most important reason for introducing and buttressing ethnic divisions was to safeguard against any collective political resistance to colonial rule. The societies that emerged in answer to the exigencies of western imperialism did not possess national unity. The only unity to speak of in these colonial territories was political.

The absence of a nation and the presence of a relatively strong state set the stage for the postindependence situation. In this as in other cases, the indigenous leaders entered the colonial state of affairs and, by and large, attempted to perpetuate it. The fact that the African governments do not preside over unified nations was tacitly acknowledged by many speakers at Fermeda. The Kenyans argued against any changes in the North Eastern Province because this would encourage moves toward autonomy among other Kenyan people, such as the Masai and the inhabitants of the coastal region. Similarly, the Ethiopians were apprehensive of any steps with respect to the Somali people in Ethiopia, since this would aggravate other religious and ethnic conflicts, such as those presently alive among the Eritrean people. What is recognized in these expressions of fear is the absence of a unified Kenyan or Ethiopian nation. What is further pointed to by these statements, and what is generally avoided in the discussion of the dispute over the Somali minority peoples, is the fact that this is not an isolated difficulty but part of the much wider question of the still undecided status of nationhood in these states.

There is, however, a new element that has been introduced or at least has been given new life by the latter-day colonialists, the indigenous leaders. Although the unity in these countries is still predominantly political, the membership of the political body tends to be composed of one or a few ethnic groups. In Kenya, for example, there is hardly any question that the Kikuyu and the Luo wield more political power than any other ethnic groups or even a combination of them. At the time of the Fermeda workshop, the all too real struggle for ethnic domination was dramatically demonstrated through widespread reports that loyalty oaths, reminiscent of the colonial Unity Oaths, were being administered among the Kikuyu in the conflicts following Tom Mboya's assassination. The fact that political power in the independent African states is held by one or two groups signifies not merely that national unity is absent, but also that political unity is based on ethnic domination.

Ethiopia has not suffered under colonialism, but the development of present-day Ethiopia since the nineteenth century displays many of the bolder features noticed in colonized Africa. A rough indication of the situation in Ethiopia can be gleaned from the Revised Constitution, the document consolidating the political unity that was the result of struggles between the people of central Ethiopia and the people inhabiting what are now the outskirts of Ethiopia for about a century. The Constitution states that Amharic, a language not spoken by a majority of the Ethiopian people, is the national language. According to the provisions of the Constitution, the office of the sovereign is to be held by the Shoan dynasty, thereby formalizing the domination of this group over other peoples of the Empire. Similarly, the Constitution makes the Orthodox Church the state religion, thereby relegating the Muslim population, which most probably constitutes a majority, to the status of second-class citizenship. The Constitution also includes many liberal articles designed to accommodate the Eritrean people, who had enjoyed certain democratic rights under the British Administration. Thus, in most of its important articles, the Constitution provides for the ethnic, religious, and regional domination of many peoples of Ethiopia. The political unity of Ethiopia is, therefore, based on manifest inequality between its various peoples.

Ethnic, religious, and regional domination—as opposed to the fact of tribal division—has not drawn the attention of Western social science. Social science, insofar as it has addressed itself to African countries, has shown its approval of political unity based on ethnic and religious domination. It commences its analysis of African countries by taking the colonial experience and its aftermath, not as the outcome of the historical acts of men, but as a natural fact of these societies. African societies are portrayed as eternally plagued with tribal conflicts. The prescription for this natural condition, then, is for these various groups to be united through political rule under a dominant group. The formation of one-party dictator-ships is applauded as a necessary prerequisite for the demands of economic development. Similarly, social scientists have been enthusiastic in their acceptance of Ethiopia's Revised Constitution. Here also Amhariza-tion, a polite term for ethnic and religious domination, is prescribed as a necessary condition of Ethiopia's mod-ernization. In this as in other cases, contemporary social science takes its point of departure from historical reali-ties that are accepted as axiomatic natural facts, and after some investigation it ends by sanctioning these same realities. The findings of social-science inves-tigations are like a conjurer's trick, since after compli-cated and manifold moves we turn up with what we started out with. What passes for rational explanation, as the distraction achieved by a conjurer's maneuvers, is merely the semblance of rational connections.

Although the methodology of social science is perplexing, it is only natural that it should reflect the political experience under which it has developed. It developed as a rationalization of advanced industrial society. It argued that the ideal or myth of pluralism has become the form of government in the advanced societies of the West. Pluralism, understood as the equitable consideration of the interests of legitimate groups, imposes two limitations: the only legitimate claims are those of groups that are in fact in power; and the only political question is the distribution of wealth among existing interests. Here again the pre-suppositions of the model of analysis rule out virtually all the significant questions at the outset. It is this reduced frame of discourse that gives rise to strange conclusions when it is faithfully applied to the African realities.

What is puzzling about the policies of these African countries and the ideology of contemporary social science is the effort to make a virtue of a crippling weakness. The political unity that prevails in these regions is based on glaring inequality between those holding political and economic power and the rest of the people, who suffer the oppression of their languages, cultures, and religions over and above their social and economic degradation. It is just the paradoxical character of this unity that becomes evident in the odd steps taken whenever the political authorities in these territories are challenged. For example, whenever the Ethiopian regime is seriously challenged, it raises the specter of Muslim hordes closing in on Ethiopia. This threat, even if real, can hardly be a salutary move toward national unity, since many of Ethiopia's peoples are Muslim. As is suggested by the futility of this gesture, to advocate political unity in a situation of ethnic and religious inequality is simply to say that the problem can be solved by perpetuating it.

It should be clear, therefore, that sovereign states or parties advocating their interests cannot offer a solution to the plight of minority peoples. Since the interests of these states can be best served through the maintenance of inequality between ethnic groups and religions, they cannot be expected to do away with their own interests. And it is not likely that social and political classes would surrender their power at the negotiating table. Since ethnic and religious domination supports the political and social order of these countries, the struggle for equality between ethnic, religious, and regional groups perforce requires struggle against these social and political orders. A lasting solution to the conflicts over minority peoples and the more general religious and ethnic divisions must proceed through the slower and more complex steps of internal social and political changes.

The Solution

The makings of a solution to the problems of minority peoples and other forms of ethnic and religious conflict can be found through a recognition of the minimum content of the principle of self-determination. This would mean, first of all, recognition of the equality of all religions. Although the recognition of this right might be difficult in particular cases, there is nothing startling about the right itself. It is merely a call for the secularization of the state. Further, self-determination would require recognition of the equality of all languages and cultures. No one has a right to infringe upon the customs, cultures, and languages of the people. It is equally essential to realize that a progressive national culture cannot be legislated into existence. Rather, a truly national culture can develop only through the free development of the progressive elements of the rich and diversified heritage of all the people. But the recognition of these rights would leave vast economic inequalities between various peoples. Unity between these various regions can be constructed only upon a high level of economic development, which would allow for socially equalizing steps such as the introduction of industry into agriculturally poor areas. Effective maintenance of this free development among diverse groups requires a measure of regional self-rule. The minimum content of the principle of self-determination thus provides for the condition whereby the people can significantly determine their own destiny. The realization of these elements of equality between ethnic, religious, and regional groups can form the basis for the development of genuine national unity.

It is obvious that, if the present regimes rest on inequality, the measures for equality contained in the minimum content of the principle of self-determination cannot be realized within these same social and political orders. Accordingly, the struggle against ethnic, religious, and regional domination can only form part of the wider struggle against social and political oppression. The danger to genuine unity within nations and between states does not lie in the struggle against ethnic, religious, and regional oppression, but in the failure to recognize the inseparable connections between these forms of oppression and those of the social and political variety.

I am not, of course, suggesting that with the fulfillment of these goals all conflicts regarding minority peoples and other ethnic and religious groups would disappear. It might be, for example, that the Somali people in Kenya and Ethiopia would still want to join the Republic of Somalia. But in these changed circumstances their quite genuine dissatisfactions, now shared by many other peoples in the same countries, would have been overcome. The call for unity then would not contain the hypocritical appeal of asking them to submit to domination. In short, the conditions for meeting problems that may still survive would be eminently propitious.

In the otherwise uncertain future of the African continent one thing is certain: the peoples of Africa will continue to struggle against social and political oppression. What I have tried to suggest, and what was overlooked by the Fermeda workshop, is that an enduring solution to other forms of oppression can be profitably sought only within the framework of a wider movement for social justice.

6. Appraisal by Three Americans

by Leonard W. Doob, William J. Foltz, and Robert B. Stevens

As the reader now knows, the three of us played a triple role at Fermeda. As organizers, we were called upon to perform various housekeeping chores that fell outside the domain of our gracious assistant. She journeyed to town literally or figuratively to buy toothpaste or socks for someone in the group and in her flawless Italian to arrange return train and air reservations; but we ourselves constantly had to make, in our adequate German, logistical decisions involving the hotel and to cope with personal problems of the participants (for example, listening during the early hours of one morning to a man who wanted to go home). In the T-groups we were participants, not bystanders; hence to a certain extent each of us endured the emotional stresses and obtained the personal insights provided by this kind of experience. Above all, we were observers; and in every spare moment, especially late at night when we were too tired to be effective, we jotted down notes, or alone in our rooms, we poured our impressions into a tape recorder. Most of what follows we composed as quickly as we could immediately after Fermeda.[1]

Expectations and Behavior

As social scientists will, we approached the workshop with partially defined expectations about the way the workshop would proceed and about possible outcomes. Our expectations were based on our own previous research, assertions made in the established literature, and our individual or joint "feel" of the situation.

Perhaps our firmest expectation was that nationality would provide the most salient principle of association, trust, and like-mindedness among the African participants. We further expected that this principle would become less salient as the workshop proceeded, and indeed we encouraged the trainers in their plan to design matters so as to "lace these people together a half-dozen different ways" and thereby encourage association on other bases. These expectations proved more nearly false than true. After the first day—in which fairly standard, although eager, "get-acquainted" procedures were evident—observable informal groups of both a substantive and recreational nature almost always included more than one nationality. Since all three national groups, with varying ease, could communicate among themselves in an indigenous language incomprehensible to nonnationals and furthermore might be expected to enjoy the relaxation and distinctiveness such communication would afford, the multinational character of the groups was particularly noteworthy. In addition to whatever links the intangibles of interpersonal sympathies might have created, we observed that international links were created on the bases of both political ideology and attitude toward the training experience. The most obvious ideological links were forged across national boundaries as a result of intellectual or emotional proclivities for some radical solution as opposed to more incremental change. In addition, at least one person from each national group was consistently interested in the workshop technique for its own sake and strongly supportive of its technical operation, and at least one was for much of the time reserved or hostile. Like ideology, these orientations carried over to create cross-cutting linkages that persisted within and outside the formal sessions.

Indeed our strongest surprise came toward the end of the first week, when for the first time participants were asked formally to caucus in national groups to accomplish a substantive task jointly with their fellow countrymen. Reluctance was widespread, affecting to some degree members of all three national groups, and two of the three groups insisted on redefining the task in a less sensitive direction once they had finally agreed to meet. Several factors, including perhaps the way the task was presented (some participants clearly resented the authoritarian nature of the directive to produce complaints) and of course the effects of the preceding "lacing," may have contributed to the reluctance. In individual conversations with us, however, participants suggested that a lack of complete trust in their fellow countrymen was a motivating factor in at least two of the national groups. When dealing with sensitive issues, many of them preferred to associate with persons with whom they could reasonably expect to have only exceptional contact once the workshop ended, even though such persons in fact might objectively be classed as enemies on the issue in question.

The avoidance of one's own national group was most evident in the case of the Kenyans, perhaps because of the high level of political tensions in Kenya following Mboya's then recent assassination, perhaps because of their background, which inclined them to behave in a less cohesive manner under most circumstances, or perhaps simply because of traits idiosyncratic to that particular group. This, too, caught us by surprise, since on the basis of the existing literature we had expected intragroup trust to be clearly lowest among the Ethiopians. As expected, the Somalis' individualism permitted them to work together easily and openly.

Rather than decreasing in strength, however, nationality became more salient at the end than at the beginning of the workshop. Two factors appeared to be at work here. First, as the discussion focused increasingly on the substantive issue and as easy compromise solutions proved inadequate, national positions became more solid and more salient in determining overall patterns of interaction. Second, something of a "reentry" phenomenon occurred during the last two days, when several individuals retreated from previously established conciliatory positions in a manner to suggest either, consciously or unconsciously, that they were preparing a safe record of suitably nationalistic statements with which to protect themselves from attack once they had returned home or, possibly, as they realized that they were about to resume their normal lives, they were reminded of the importance of nationalistic symbols.

Other expectations related to mechanisms through which the African participants might build interpersonal solidarity among themselves or avoid direct confrontation with the substantive issues dividing them. One such mechanism likely to be particularly useful in a stressful context in which non-Africans were exercising at least limited authority would be the building of solidarity on the basis of antiwhite sentiments. Contrary to our expectations, at no point was such sentiment mobilized. Other participants greeted the only such attempt with embarrassment and hostility. A few individuals, particularly in the early days, did make punishing remarks about whites generally, but these were made in passing and were not picked up by the group. Specific condemnations of acts or policies of specific groups of whites were frequent but were usually not misplaced, nor did they betray any latent purpose.

A second expected mechanism, evident in many formal inter-African meetings particularly of major political leaders, was the avoidance of conflicts of substance in favor of utopian appeals to eventual political unity of all Africa. This was much in evidence. In each of the two T-groups, and even more so in the General Assembly, participants would attempt to avoid or soften points of stress by emphasizing that all would be worked out "in the framework of the unity which we all seek." Alternatively, the positions were phrased in terms of some blind adherence to a slogan of "federation now." The mechanism served two distinct purposes: to avoid current concrete problems whose discussion might lead to disharmony within the group and, perhaps more subtly, to soften conflictual assertions by reassuring one's opponent that opposition was only temporary and that nothing personal was implied, since the speaker would be happy to share citizenship with his opponent and all his relatives.

One further (and unexpected) mechanism of cross-national solidarity was a willingness to criticize one's own government. This openness created solidarity by putting many participants in a similar stance and so removing the speaker from direct responsibility for any of his nation's hurtful actions toward other participants' fellow citizens. As with the attitudes toward African unity, we cannot assess the sincerity or depth of these feelings by those who expressed them—much less their legitimacy—nor can we draw any conclusions about connections between overt statements, internalized attitudes, and any concrete action that might be taken on the basis of these attitudes. At this point we merely note the functions they performed in the workshop context.

Formal Group Processes and Problems

Each of the two matched T-groups developed strong group loyalties and pride at moving faster and more productively than the other. Occasional visitors from the other group were treated as interlopers. In classic style, the T-groups began in confusion, proceeded to frustration, and on the third day suddenly coalesced to conduct an impressive and profitable discussion without benefit of formal leadership or agenda. Succeeding sessions were even better, though both groups eventually returned to some semblance of the initial frustration during the first sessions in which the border dispute was discussed directly. After that, one T-group made notably greater progress than the other: brainstorming sessions were more serious and productive; the disputes were examined more carefully and with less avoidance behavior; the solutions proposed were more specific; and the group stood more solidly behind its own recommendations. The difference is most simply, and perhaps sufficiently, explained by the presence in the laggard group of an individual whose aggressive, uncontrolled behavior, often exacerbated by drink, seemed most probably to be idiosyncratically, not culturally, determined. That group never developed a means of reducing or neutralizing his erratic and sometimes calculatedly disruptive behavior, which seemed to manifest itself most when some progress or agreement was close to hand.

The more effective T-group contained two persons who never became constructively involved, but their deviance took the form of nonparticipation. One of these men was a last-minute recruit and was possibly inadequately briefed about what to expect. He attended sessions regularly but passively and was made obviously uncomfortable by any attempts to bring him into discussions. Such attempts eventually ceased. The second of these misfits arrived five days late and then spent more time sleeping and playing cards with guests at the inn than participating in the workshop. His occasional contributions, while valuable in content, had limited impact because of his failure to participate in the early sessions. Although at times distressing to the organizers, and some of the Africans, the silent deviants in that T-group proved nondisruptive, and the group learned to function effectively without their contributions.

In contrast to the T-groups' general success was the weakness of the General Assembly. Only rarely were these larger discussions productive. Avoidance behavior, intransigence, and various forms of posturing and undercutting, which had earlier been overcome in the T-groups, reappeared in the General Assembly. One procedural sign of difficulty was the General Assembly's stifling reliance on formal parliamentary procedure, which reasserted its grip despite repeated and seemingly unanimous efforts to follow freer styles of discussion. Somehow the pompous parliamentary atmosphere—analogous to that which many of the participants derided in their own national parliaments—became so compelling that even the organizers found themselves rising deferentially before Mr. Chairman to a point of order, personal privilege, or the like.

Rather than a cause of the General Assembly's difficulties, the exacerbated parliamentarism seems more a reaction to them, a largely ineffective way to cope with real procedural problems. Among the problems, again, was the disruptive figure mentioned earlier, who in the General Assembly had new and broader fields to disrupt. Certainly his presence in the General Assembly was a major reason why most of the members of the more productive T-group sought to avoid plenary sessions. Further, of course, conducting a chairmanless nondirected meeting of twenty-one people is more difficult than conducting one with ten persons. The trainers felt, in retrospect, that a different design that would have placed more emphasis on sensitivity training in the plenary session, rather than the T-groups, could have overcome the difficulty. While this opinion cannot be proved by our experience, the view is given some credence by the remarkable similarity of speech patterns in the final General Assembly sessions to those present in the T-groups a week earlier, before the effect of training had been felt. Even so, the creation of effective communication and interpersonal trust in the larger group might well have required more time than the workshop allowed.

The workshop, in sum, confirmed the old dictum that the expression of attitude depends in part upon the situation at hand. Again and again we witnessed instances of the same person's inconsistently expressing, for example, conciliatory views in his T-group and then being silent or defending a more rigid position in the General Assembly. National groups caucused without Americans present, but our informal reports suggest that this context also influenced expression, as well as content. Perhaps the T-groups succeeded too well and thereby prevented the participants from transferring their emotional attachments either to the General Assembly or to the national groups.

Attitudes and Opinions

We have obtained some sense of the attitudes and opinions of the participants on the two disputes in question from the documents the nationals of each country composed in response to the request to list their grievances and to anticipate the grievances of their opponents as well as from our observations of views expressed in the T-groups, the General Assembly, and informal conversations.

One point is clearer than all the rest: the Somalis were well acquainted beforehand with the arguments and values of the Kenyans and Ethiopians, and vice versa. For example, the Somalis anticipated that the Ethiopians would claim that "Ethiopia is a heterogeneous state and cannot admit ethnic separatist movements"; while the Ethiopians said the Somalis failed "to appreciate the far-reaching consequences of redrawing African boundary lines (*a*) through the advancement of linguistic and ethnic ties as a basis of nationhood, and (*b*) through the rejection of existing borders." At the same time some of the issues were probably more salient than others, or the participants may have been reluctant to express them. Thus the Somalis in their written document did not perceive that the Kenyans might describe Somalia as "being looked at by Russia as a stepping-stone to Eastern Africa and therefore being substantially armed."

The three of us also submitted a document to the General Assembly in which we tried to anticipate, on the basis of our knowledge of the countries, the grievances each side would express. One noteworthy fact about our lists was that virtually every item was independently mentioned by the participants. This we take to be further evidence of the common knowledge concerning the border disputes that educated and informed persons, whether Africans or non-Africans, share. In addition we, unlike the Africans, did not hesitate to describe the stereotypes frequently held by the nationals of each of these countries about the inhabitants of the other two. Significantly, there was no disagreement with our characterization.

Both in the documents and in the discussions there were few disputes over facts. Obviously there could be no argument about the role of the European powers in dividing and governing the Horn in accordance with the treaties they had enforced upon themselves and the African peoples there. That the majority of the persons in the disputed areas are Somalis, ethnically and linguistically, was not subject to debate. More surprising, however, was assent to facts that in other international conflicts are likely to produce charges and counter-charges, such as the offensive quality of the propaganda broadcast from the Somali radio stations or the brutal treatment of some Somalis by the Ethiopian and Kenyan army and police. The facts could be accepted, but the evaluation differed markedly.

The most critical difference in evaluation involved the issues of self-determination and sovereignty. The Somalis never retreated from their view that "the inhabitants of these areas [have the right] to determine their own fate" nor the Kenyans and the Ethiopians from their position that each of them is a nation defined, in the words of the former, as "a people [having] a defined territorial border [and] a recognized political structure [with] legal authority, internationally recognized political boundaries, [and] territorial integrity." These were the most intensely held attitudes, and almost always whenever affect was expressed, the clash was between the two irreconciliable positions.

The workshop and informal conversations could not probe more deeply to uncover the reasons for the strength of these values. If we asked a Somali why he felt so strongly about the people of the Ogaden, he would either consider the question slightly insane or he would mention relatives of his who reside there or shrines and waterholes needed by his people. The Kenyans and the Ethiopians were equally surprised when asked why it mattered whether or not the territories were retained: they could supply economic reasons, they could mention treaty rights, they could stress the possibility of other ethnic groups also wanting to leave their multiracial states, but most of all they expressed incredulity that anyone would even wonder why a government would be unwilling to relinquish its sovereign rights. "What is in it for us?" the Kenyans and Ethiopians asked again and again when confronted with proposals that buffer zones be created within or outside the disputed areas. In a sense the overriding symbol that had reality for these men was land: land for grazing, land belonging to the tribe or the nation, tangible land. Although they may have used the fashionable jargon of the times, especially the phrase "national identity," they really attached deep emotional significance to the concepts and extrapolated very easily from personal or tribal concepts of land and property to attribute such concepts to the modern African state.

All of us experienced the intensity of feeling expressed especially toward the end of the workshop. But cracks also appeared in the national armor. Anecdotes were slipped in that had a less absolutist tone; it is such a nuisance, one man remarked, to have to stop driving when the national flag is being raised or lowered: It may be, some of the participants said, that we have to sacrifice some of our sovereignty to attain peace; or perhaps some of the history is not relevant to the present problem; or we must also consider the circumstances under which plebiscites or other forms of self-determination should be encouraged.

A set of values that did not change was the willingness to criticize one's own government. One man in a T-group stated that he would be critical at home but not abroad, yet he was soon joined by the other participants in pointing out the abuses to which he and others are subjected. Sometimes it was even suggested that the governments had a vested interest in continuing the border disputes in order to distract people's attention from domestic problems; at other times it was stated openly that no solution for the disputes could possibly be achieved under the present regimes. It is doubtful whether such views would have been expressed if the participants had been questioned directly, for we had sought out men whose opinions might be listened to by government. We now know that the government connections do exist but that any group of intellectuals in these countries is likely to express attitudes some of which are critical of the status quo without, however, being unpatriotic or disloyal. One participant, in fact, rose and accused the others of "betraying" their countries because in his view they were making no greater progress toward solving the disputes than the governments whose views they were criticizing. Obviously each side learned something about this critical stance inside the other countries.

We hold the tentative opinion, therefore, that no fundamental changes were wrought directly by the work-

shop but that new political, economic, and social facts
may well have been learned. The participants certainly
had the opportunity to discover that their antagonists,
with the exception of very few, were men of goodwill
who subscribed to opposing viewpoints with an intensity and conviction as strong as their own. It is this
insight that may possibly have repercussions and produce change—eventually.

Proposing Solutions

Even more central to the workshop's purpose than
changing participants' attitudes was the joint exploration and prescription of solutions for the border disputes. Each of the T-groups argued through and eventually proposed a detailed solution to the disputes, and
each of the two proposals received the general assent of
the members of the T-group responsible. The emotional
and intellectual involvement of T-group members with
their joint product was strikingly intense; even the disruptive individual subscribed to his group's proposals.
At this short remove from the event it is yet impossible
to know how much of that involvement represented cal-
culated appreciation of the worth of one's labors, how
much represented pride in and support for one's T-
group, and how much it represented just the exhilaration of having finally gotten something on paper.
Although national-interest bargaining was sharp within
the T-groups, support for the proposals as they finally
emerged was apparently genuinely international.

One T-group, largely at the insistence of one of its
strongest and most useful members (a non-Somali),
began with the affirmation of the right to self-determination of the peoples in the area under dispute,

though this statement was somewhat attenuated by the affirmation that "it is a right to be exercised only under specified circumstances." The other group had repeatedly reached an impasse on the self-determination issue (it was seen as a subtle Somali device for dismembering Ethiopia and Kenya) and had carefully avoided any statement of general principles of the sort. Both proposals provided for some form of joint administration of the "disputed areas" for an interim period, with the question of sovereignty over the areas held, nonprejudicially, in abeyance. Various alternate definitions of the "disputed areas" and of the means and time for terminating the neutralization arrangements were advanced. Each proposal insisted on demilitarization of the disputed areas, with law and order being made the responsibility of a local police independent of direct control by any of the three nations. Both proposals foresaw some role for an expanded East African Community or other formal political arrangements among the three parties as part of a permanent solution.

Under extreme time pressure, the joint Planning Group, which in the second week had taken over the planning of the sessions, amalgamated the two proposals into one for presentation on the last day to the General Assembly. This shotgun wedding of what had been the products of subtly different group processes did not, alas, produce a well-integrated child. One example of the difficulties of the compromise was the reappearance of a deus ex machina role for political unity of the three nations as the sole way of effecting a permanent solution for the border dispute. In retrospect, it is easy to see that the amalgamation of the two documents was a major tactical mistake. When the combined document was presented to the General Assembly, it seemed to satisfy no one, and the whole group reached a frustrating and infuriating stalemate. The principal reasons included disappointment at seeing one's original ideas, product of so much arduous thought and negotiation in the T-group, modified or omitted in the compromise document: "What I see here is that my group's document has been adulterated!" The reentry phenomenon also played its part: "As time goes by here, I am becoming more reluctant to agree that part of our country should be given up." The difficulty of communication in the General Assembly was very much in evidence. The disrupter was his usual unhelpful self—he reversed his usual revolutionary and anti-European stance to quote, approvingly, Churchill in favor of absolute defense of territorial integrity of one's possessions—but even had he been absent in these final meetings, the other problems would have remained.

The sticking point was reached over the definition of the areas to be neutralized in the interim period, particularly over whether or not the Somali Republic would have to include some of its own territory in the "neutralized zone." On the one hand, Somalis could claim with perfect accuracy that there was no dispute over any territory now part of the Somali Republic and that it would be senseless to introduce dispute where none existed. On the other hand, Kenyans and Ethiopians could claim perfectly reasonably that all parties to the dispute would have to give up something in any reasonable compromise and that the Somalis just seemed to be looking for something for nothing. "What is it that the Somalis really want?" one participant kept repeating. The various elaborate proposals for resolving or avoiding the issue that had been worked out in the T-groups were rejected in the General Assembly. Yet if some of the national stereotypes were again conjured up, even at the most heated moments, it was clear that national lines did not hold entirely firm. T-group loyalty, ideological proclivity, and newfound intellectual conviction cut across national boundaries to produce smaller groupings of like-minded men on specific issues.

Thus the Fermeda workshop did not end with a final communique proposing a single peace formula and signed happily by all; but it did produce general agreement on a two-stage approach involving neutralization of disputed areas during the initial period.

Summary

The reader must share some of our ambivalence about the Fermeda workshop—and possibly some of our exhilaration and some of our frustrations.

One success cannot be questioned except by those who did not have to endure our travail: the workshop took place, all the African participants arrived, the governments voiced no objection, competent trainers were obtained, and we were able to keep our promise of providing a permissive atmosphere in which any view could be expressed. We had no authority, and until the very end no funds, to compel these people to gamble their time and come to Fermeda. Private initiative through university connections was sufficient. In addition, the participants certainly became acquainted with one another and in many instances, we surmise, formed strong friendships across national lines. They expressed to themselves and to us the basic grievances of the countries regarding the border disputes and in this manner revealed their attitudes and values.

From a research point of view, we believe the tech-

nique revealed attitudes and complex cognitive processes not obtainable through more standard ques-
tioning techniques; but the workshop inevitably involved only a small sample of persons, and data have
been derived in a form that makes coding extremely
difficult. The lack of a control group was unavoidable.
Finally, the fact that the sample's composition is sure to
be known to the governments concerned poses confi-
dentiality problems of a very high order. Against such
difficulties in using the technique as a research tool, one
clearcut advantage stands out, particularly when dealing
with a group like ours. In contrast to the usual relation
between researcher and subject—which is increasingly resented in the developing nations as a subtle form of
"academic imperialism"—no information was available
to us that was not equally available to the African participants and, should they so choose, to their governments as well. More so than anything we may write, it
will be through the African participants' public and private communications that the Fermeda workshop will
have its greatest impact.

On the other hand, the main objective of the workshop, at least on the surface, was certainly not achieved.
No original solution to the disputes was evolved that
won the instant acclaim of all the participants.

We equally have no way of knowing definitely
whether the successes and the failures of the workshop,
whatever they were, can be attributed to the use of
sensitivity training and the various techniques that our
valued trainers employed. As already noted, there was
no control group—and perforce there could be none—to
ascertain whether the mere congregating of three groups
of sincere African scholars atop a Tyrolean mountain
would have produced the same, better, or worse results

if they had begun discussing the substantive issues immediately, without the delay that such training entailed. Lectures and games were infrequently referred to in subsequent sessions, but this fact does not mean that a residue therefrom had no effect upon the men's behavior.

We venture the opinion, the guess, the clinical judgment that the training did contribute appreciably to the breaking down of reserve and to the enhancing of communication between participants from different nations. It is possible that, in the absence of the disrupter and of the tension resulting from the assassination of Tom Mboya, the more laggard of the T-groups and the General Assembly itself might have made greater progress. We cannot, we repeat, prove these statements of faith, we can only express confidence in them. On the other hand, the genial atmosphere created by the scenery around Fermeda, by the drinking, by the card playing, and perhaps by the T-groups may have encouraged the participants to be polite to one another and in this way to avoid, rather than face head on, the complicated issues. Our presence—scholars from the West with white skins—may have been inhibiting, although several participants told us they appreciated non-African auspices.

In the future, if the Fermeda technique is to prove useful in other conflicts, we believe that the participants must make a firmer commitment than we were able to procure to support and carry through with the procedural requirements a workshop imposes. No hard sell should be applied by enthusiastic organizers. Participants must want to come and must want to get the dispute settled badly enough to sacrifice some personal dignity and to make substantive concessions. We might also favor a more authoritarian reg-

imen for the entire enterprise, including the right to
reject participants.

The possibility of another Fermeda suggests other procedural changes. We now realize that most of our African participants—though some more than others—
resisted any attempt in the T-groups to probe too
deeply into personal style or behavior; but we remain
convinced that some probing is necessary. Obviously
there is no rigid rule that tells how deep to go; the
trainers, the organizers, and the participants must take
their cue from the persons at hand and the questions at
issue. For the moment we most tentatively think that
the sharp temporal distinction we drew between training
in behalf of developing self-awareness and, more especially, communication skills on the one hand and the
discussion of the substantive issues may have been a
mistake and ought, therefore, to be blurred in the future. The Africans who might be invited to workshops
have usually had to struggle hard to reach an elite status
in their countries, and they must rip themselves away
from their normal routines to participate; consequently
they are likely to be impatient or affronted when at the
outset they find themselves in an unstructured, leaderless group having, from their standpoint, no immediately obvious connection with the objective that has
brought them together. It would therefore perhaps be
better to begin a workshop with the substantive issue as
the thesis and to let personal probing creep in slowly
but inevitably as the antithesis. Achieving a synthesis
under these conditions would probably take more than
two weeks, a fact that in turn might require other modi-
fications in procedure. Intermittent meetings over a
longer period, for example, if feasible, would enable the
men to move back and forth between T-groups and the

real life of their professions and government. These suggestions and those appearing in virtually every chapter of this book indicate clearly the need for innovation, and we must struggle on.

As social scientists, we are somewhat dissatisfied with the subjectivity and untested reliability of many observations made by the trainers and by us during Fermeda and in this book. Such informality seems unavoidable: they were always weighed down by their responsibility to provide leadership and advice, we performed simultaneously the three roles mentioned at the start of this chapter, and all of us eventually grew physically and emotionally weary. In retrospect, nevertheless, we feel that we might have been able to "measure"—the word is enclosed in quotation marks to try to make it sound a little less pretentious—a number of the changes that were or were not occurring during the two weeks. If this had been done, at the time we might conceivably have had better insight into our progress or lack of it; and we certainly would have emerged with more concrete data, not to impress our other academic colleagues, but to transmit what we think we learned at Fermeda. For this reason, consequently, we offer in Appendix 4 a catalogue of unobtrusive measures that might have been used and in Appendix 5, for what it is worth, the results from a questionnaire that was actually distributed to the participants.

Should Fermeda be repeated? Aside from the obvious point that, as of this writing, the dispute has not been solved even to the satisfaction of three groups of influential intellectuals, other limitations on the future use of the technique must be spelled out. First, such a workshop is not an inexpensive undertaking; the Fermeda costs ran to about $40,000, not including many hidden expenses including salaries and overheads absorbed by Yale over an extended period. Secondly, a workshop is very time-consuming, and it is difficult to find men of the required caliber who can give up a particular two weeks of their lives. The time involved for the organizers before, during, and after the workshop at least equals that spent on any major research effort. Should the organizers be so foolish as to start such a venture from scratch and take on the responsibility of arousing interest on the part of participants, governments, and foundations, they may find the effort disproportionate to any conceivable result. A moderately financed non-government machine, therefore, is needed to manage the details and to provide funds painlessly and quickly as the need and opportunity arise.

We conclude by restating the obvious: the travail, the time, and the expense are all of little importance if a Fermeda type of workshop contributes even marginally to the settlement of a major international dispute.

7. Appraisal by a Trainer

by Charles K. Ferguson

The writer was one of four trainers recruited by the Yale organizers to serve as staff for the Fermeda workshop. While background among the four differed, we had in common a great deal of applied familiarity with the use of experience-based learning groups (T-groups, laboratory groups, sensitivity-training groups, encounter groups, human relations groups, and the like) in varied settings, and we shared a commitment to the educational value of such groups, properly employed, as instruments for learning, for change, for the development of significant relationships, and for exploration and problem solving.

For anyone concerned with human systems, Fermeda was a great opportunity. Behavioral scientists have had ample opportunity to work with human systems of all sizes from a single person (in counseling and psychotherapy) to small groups (in team building, group therapy, group dynamics) to large organizations, industries, governmental units, communities, and so on (in organizational development). There has been, however, almost no opportunity to have access to international problems or to a human system involving several nations as subsystems.

It is evident that the pathologies of each larger system affect the life and adjustment of smaller subordinate systems. Just as family pathology and problems affect its individual members, the community affects the family, the society affects the community, the industry affects its divisions, and the nation affects the state, so the relationship among nations affects all within that complex. With increasing interdependence attending the development of communications, transportation, and nuclear and hydrogen energy, pathologies in international relations jeopardize all, everywhere. The Fermeda workshop presented a unique opportunity to apply some of what we have learned from cumulative experience with smaller systems to an international human system involving problems in the relations among people of several sovereign nations. There are probably no problems of greater social consequence.

Simply stated, our goal at Fermeda was to develop among diverse people with differing loyalties significant relationships and a collaborative set that might sustain the solution of thorny, emotionally laden problems relating to the borders of their countries and the lives of their countrymen.

The laboratory method was suitable to this goal because it is known that a T-group can produce strong, positive, rewarding, and sustaining personal relationships in a relatively short period. A T-group begins with minimal structure, without specified agenda, and without conventional leadership. In the process of finding its way, of building structure, of constructing an agenda, a T-group develops an appreciation for the individuality and idiosyncrasies of its members, a common history mutually perceived by the members, and a bonding of relationship based upon the shared experience of creating something from virtually nothing and then of having lived together through the conflicts and satisfactions that inevitably attend that process and link the people who share in it.

The Background

Fermeda was implemented in 1969 in a context of painful memories of failure to bring off the workshop the year before. This led to considerable anxiety regarding the hazards and the success of the venture. Quite a few fears infected the staff, some realistic and some, as it turned out, unrealistic. It was actively feared, for instance, that an appreciable number of participants, or even a country's total delegation, might not arrive for the workshop—in fact, all came. It was also feared that hostilities might run so deep and personal controls be so tenuous that violent physical confrontation might occur between participants. Though no such encounters took place, the fear was unsettling. It was feared, in a less disturbing way, that suspicion, dislike, and distrust of a white-American staff might be a major problem. There was, in fact, an attempt by one participant to mobilize antiwhite feeling, but it drew no support. Staff anxiety was compounded by the complexity of the logistics (people coming from farflung parts of the world), the enormous and time-consuming effort and energy that had gone into promoting the venture, the uniqueness and experimental nature of the opportunity, and the additional uneasiness caused by the fact that prior to arrival in Italy no member of the sponsoring Yale group had ever personally met any of the four trainers to whom they were entrusting a venture in which they had invested so much. And the trainers, though they had professional ties, were in essence a pick-up team from scattered parts of the USA that had not had the benefit of time to integrate in preparation for this specific venture. It is no wonder that we approached the workshop, with all these unknowns and uncertainties, as though it were fragile.

It is possible, because of the cautiousness our sense of fragility produced, that we were too delicate in our contact; that we did not work out the process problems in the total group courageously enough; in short, that we did not do full enough justice to the method. It may have been like driving in a nail but being so fearful of driving it sideways that one does not strike it hard enough to insert it all the way.

Another aspect that affected the venture had to do with participant recruitment and selection. Because the workshop's cancellation the previous year had disappointed and angered many recruits, and because the opportunity to realize the plans in 1969 had developed late, there had to be a crash effort to recruit substitute participants. As a result some participants were not helpful in moving toward the goals of the workshop. One person was so self-oriented and so demanding that he represented a significant liability to the workshop and did in fact hinder its development materially. One person lacked the understanding, sympathy and/or social skills to participate at all effectively; he was frustrated and ineffective throughout the workshop. One person was either too unaware of and/or too uncommitted to the workshop method to be used; he represented a major hindrance in early stages, although in later stages he was a productive member. One person from each of the three countries was in a poor position to exert influence at home: one worked in another African country (though he spent his holidays at home); a second was on his way to the United States for three months; and a third—after returning to Africa at the end of the workshop—spent half a year sabbatical in the United States. Two persons used alcohol in a way that negatively affected the workshop.

Evaluation

From observation at Fermeda it appeared that we both succeeded and failed.

We succeeded in producing positive relationships within each of the two T-groups that did evoke sufficient collaboration to yield agreement regarding the border problems. The solutions of the two groups differed, but there was collaboration and commitment within each group. We failed when we tried to put the two groups together to get one commonly agreed-upon solution.

We succeeded because we devoted enough time within T-groups for members to go through the necessary phases in a process of group development that involves the discovery and working through of conflict required for the linking of people, for development of trust, for mutual understanding and respect, and for resolution of some differences. T-group members learned to use each other as resources; to enjoy each other; to feel anger at and affection for each other; to identify with each other; to care; to invest in each other; to build a small society in which each had a stake; to find, share, and explore their uniqueness as individuals and as representatives of different cultures; and, importantly, to find and explore their essential humanity, their similarities, their samenesses, and their superordinate goals as human beings.

We failed in the total group because we did not allow enough time nor did we work through the conflict and process problems necessary in the phases of group growth to develop a useful vehicle out of the total group. In addition, hindsight tells us that we should have known that the success of the two small groups and commitment by each to its product would make the integration of the two products and two groups into one product and one group that much more difficult.[1]

Factors contributing to the results at Fermeda include the ways in which attitudes were mobilized and relationships developed. Human attitudes have range; we all carry the capacity for like-dislike, love-hate, cooperate-resist, and support-oppose. Most of us are sufficiently complicated to have available multiple attitudes, or shadings of attitude, toward any one phenomenon. It was apparent that the African participants were entirely human in this respect. Among the Kenyans, ambivalent-multivalent attitudes were evident on many fronts between participants who were Kikuyu and Luo, between Masai and Kikuyu-Luo, between Kamba and the others. Tribal, national, African, and international identification competed within each person, causing ambivalence regarding the self. Among the Ethiopians the same multiplicity was apparent between those who were Amharas, Tigres, and Muslims. Among Somalis, ambivalence appeared less sharply but nevertheless quite clearly, because of primary tribal identification, degree of dedication to Islam, personal distance from a nomadic way of life, and so forth. These Africans were, as all people are, capable of defining themselves differently in response to different circumstances at different times. Their resistance was mobilized, but so was their cooperation.

In the workshop relationships were developed, altered, and clarified among participants from the same country and between participants from different countries. For example, a Somali—who had been raised in what is now Ethiopia and who stated that he had been taught actively to hate the Amhara as oppressive to Ethiopia and Somali—came to reevaluate his attitude and to change his feelings because of contact in the workshop with Amhara who did not fit his prior stereotype. People were linked occupationally across borders. They discovered mutual attitudes about many things—for example, women, politics, values, and traditions. They also, of course, discovered differences not only across boundaries but within each country. An important difference concerned the cultural orientation toward the meaning of land. For nomadic Somalis a significant value is the freedom to move from place to place in order to seek favorable sites in terms of rain and grazing opportunities; they are not attached to a particular piece of land. For Kenyans and Ethiopians the value is just the opposite: they prize the freedom to own land, to be identified with a specific area. Freedom to move as against freedom to remain fixed—this difference was philosophically explored and more completely understood.

On the other hand, differences appeared within each country, and greater identification often seemed to exist between representatives of the three national groups than among members of the same national group. Ethiopians split over the degree of dedication to the principle of self-determination. There was a similar split among the Somalis over the willingness to contribute some of their land to a border-buffer zone. The Somalis were also divided concerning the importance of perpetuating a nomadic way of life, concerning Muslim orthodoxy, and concerning the individual's obligation to his tribe. Differences among the Kenyans were plentiful; not only were there clear tribal splits and rivalries, but there were also differences in personal style and conduct, politics, original language and culture, and the like.

In the T-group situation, in short, we succeeded because the collaborative, cooperative impulses in personalities were mobilized and released as a result of the situation itself, the size of each group (twelve or thirteen), and the allocated time (a solid week). But we failed with the same participants in the General Assembly because competition, noncooperation, caginess, resistance, and hostility were mobilized as a result of that situation (a formal one, in which there was no provision for the building and repairing of relationships), the size of the group (twenty-five—too large for the available time), and the allocated time (too short).*

Though we succeeded and failed, it was established that a venture such as this one can be successful if by success is meant that from among man's multiple impulses, his attitudes and relationships leading to constructive collaboration and problem-solving can be mobilized. The task is not easy, but we know a good deal about how to arrange conditions that will elicit collaboration. Fermeda established that it is possible among multinational groups to evoke meaningful collaboration on difficult problems of conflicting national interest.

How do we know that the same or better results would not have been achieved without T-groups, with other methods, or from the same group simply by being together for a similar length of time? We do not know absolutely of course. But we can reason from experience with other intergroup problems in large organizations

---

*The contrasts between parliamentary and leaderless groups in general and between the T-groups and the General Assembly at Fermeda are also described and presented in greater detail in Appendix 3 by William J. Crockett, one of the four trainers at Fermeda.—Ed.

that seriously competitive problems between groups do not cure themselves. While attitudes are reversible, catalytic influence is needed to change them. The T-group is among the most powerful human catalytic social inventions of recent time. There may be other effective catalysts, but the writer knows of none with greater promise for exacerbating and working through conflict in a context within which the released energy can be constructively and creatively used for learning and/or problem solving.

The T-group is an effective instrument for many reasons.[2] It replicates in microcosm the dynamics of the real system without acting it out. It focuses on an examination of its own process, analyzing and learning from what is happening right here and now. It provides an instrument to "see" problems or divisions between people more clearly because they are projected and illustrated in the group and to accelerate the search for solutions that personal and shared identification with problems stimulates. Rooted attitudes of hostility do not suddenly give way to cooperative ones without some intervening variable, some catalyst. Fermeda provided evidence that it is possible for a T-group to be the catalyst that can produce a satisfactory level of collaboration among representatives from hostile states.

Suggestions for the Future

If the Fermeda workshop were to be repeated, our goals would be the same: to develop significant and positive relationships among participants that would bear the stress of difficult problems; and to mobilize attitudes that produce effective collaboration and problem solving. Our method as it involved the T-group would be the same.

But in my view, we would do some things differently if we could control them. We would be more careful in the selection of participants with respect to their readiness to participate in a laboratory approach to problem-solving and to their emotional maturity. One seriously self-oriented person can drain energy and require time that handicaps the whole enterprise. We would try to recruit powerful figures within their own countries, who could immediately influence change if their attitudes altered. It would be preferable to have participants come as individuals without obligation, as these participants did, but maximum leverage for short-term problem solution might require participants in central positions of influence in their countries. This kind of participant was not fully enough represented at Fermeda.

There are other points to be remembered. Excessive alcohol is a handicap to effective work; we would try to recruit participants known to be moderate or reasonable in their drinking habits. We would work more at understanding, assisting, and building national teams, possibly even before they came to the workshop. This applies also to the American organizers, who necessarily had to integrate as a team as they went along. We would hope for greater lead and planning time. We would be less anxious, because our experience indicates that the venture was not as fragile as we feared. We failed a bit in each of the foregoing respects.

In many important ways, however, we succeeded:

1. We provided a fresh model for an approach to the solution of international problems that can be studied, replicated, adapted, modified, or rejected. We have

established a landmark, a reference point that in some measure can guide the next venturer.

2. We have linked nationals of three countries in a way they have never been linked before, and we have created new pathways across borders between people. We have to some degree accelerated social change relevant to this workshop between participants from the same countries and among participants from different countries.

3. We produced two carefully considered plans for solution of the border problems between the countries. These plans, while different, have much in common; they are now available and between them must contain much of the nub of an eventual equitable settlement.

4. We provided a vehicle that rallied the sincere energies of many men to seek a solution for the kind of international problems that have caused untold human suffering all through history. That kind of energy must be rallied often again.

8. Strategic Issues in Designing Workshops

by Richard E. Walton

The Fermeda workshop represents a significant innovation in nonformal diplomacy, though similar approaches to conflict resolution and problem solving have occurred in other institutional settings. When I assess the Fermeda design and formulate generalizations about such workshops, therefore, I am also drawing upon participation in or familiarity with dialogue and problem-solving workshops in many other settings such as: the interface between a foreign contractor and a US project management team monitoring a very large construction project; union-management relations; and interracial projects.

I want to alert the reader to an assumption and intention of mine in writing this chapter. Since I assume that similar workshops focused on international disputes will be conducted in the future—the method simply has too much potential not to be used again—I intend not only to supply some relevant experience from Fermeda, but also to suggest the general principles that should be considered in designing future workshops.

Within the basic concept underlying the Fermeda workshop there are many design options. Some decisions—such as time, duration, place, composition of participants and staff—must be made well in advance of the actual workshop. Other issues must be decided, at least tentatively, by the time the workshop gets under way. These include the initial groupings of participants and a

Support for this study was provided by the Division of Research, Harvard Graduate School of Business Administration, Soldiers Field, Boston.

plan providing for the nature and sequence of activities that are likely to achieve a number of objectives. They should yield insight into personal relationships and build up such relationships; and they should stimulate the evolution of alternate solutions to the substantive problems as well as decisions concerning those problems. Further, the differentiated roles, if any, among participants and staff must be considered. Another design question involves the selection and articulation of the operational goals to be pursued by the end of the workshop.

A major issue, which overshadows many of the above, is whether the workshop is seen as a singular event or is conceived as an element of a larger continuing project.

Composition

Intellectual and Emotional Attributes

For Fermeda to be effective, it was important for the majority of the six participants from each country to be bright, articulate, and emotionally mature. Although these ingredients were appreciated in advance, their significance was driven home by the Fermeda experience. The generally high level of intelligence and verbal skills of the participants—together with the fact that they represented a diverse set of disciplines, including political science, economics, law, education, and sociology— produced an extraordinarily high quality of discussion of the secondary and primary issues when these were the agenda during the middle period of the workshop.

The emotional maturity and interpersonal styles of participants were equally important, principally because of their potentially negative impact on the process. The format of the workshop encouraged openness about one's feelings as well as thoughts, but some persons are more comfortable than others when experiencing the expression of affect—love, hate, rejection, anger, regret, shame, guilt, hope, despair, compassion, disappointment. Those who were more threatened by such feelings—and who tended to suppress or deny such feelings in themselves and others—were less able to take advantage of the unique opportunities afforded by the workshop to engage in authentic communication and to quickly build interpersonal trust. The effect of inhibited participants at Fermeda was to slow the rate of development of strong, flexible, and trusting working groups. But such persons were relatively few, and the fact was that, by the midpoint in the workshop, two strong self-governing groups had developed. However, while intellectual skills and interpersonal styles can affect the pace and quality of the process, the presence of even one person who lacks emotional maturity and who has abnormally high self-oriented needs—for example, for attention or to be counterdependent—can seriously distort, even completely disrupt, a workshop. In the Fermeda workshop self-oriented needs of at least one member did significantly distort the functioning of one working group and the General Assembly.

Information and Interest in the Issues

Two participants did not appear to have a sufficient interest in the dispute to make the high level of emotional and intellectual investment the workshop required.

The participants, whose normal roles in society did not necessarily give them much familiarity with the history of the dispute or with facts about the area in question, were uneven in their background knowledge. There were some complaints by participants that this limitation—which tended to affect negatively the ability of some to appraise various action steps—could have been overcome by supplying the participants in advance with background reading material (to which participants from each country could have contributed).

Degree of Governmental Association

Because the problem-solving processes of the workshop require an exploratory stance, the participants selected should not be obliged to advance their government's current position on the issues. But because the process and/or products of the workshop must also be communicated to the respective governments, it is desirable to include members of the elite who have the confidence of their government. One should therefore seek some optimal level of association with the current governments. In this respect the Fermeda participants were generally appropriate for this first workshop of its kind, although it was my impression that the Kenyan participants may have had less potential influence with their government than the participants from Ethiopia and especially Somalia. In the future, with more confidence in the workshop concept, with increased knowledge of its functioning, and within the context of a favorable diplomatic trend (such as existed between Somalia and her two neighbors during 1967-69), I would encourage sponsors to aim for participants closer to the centers of power in their respective countries.

Relations among Members of a National Group

A question that arose at Fermeda deserves some attention here: If the workshop premise is that individuals are acting on the basis of their own views, opinions, and insights rather than representing a government, why should we be concerned about the quality of relations among members of the national group? The value of the team is not to insure that its members can develop a common position and a coordinated strategy of influence, a capacity that would be considered desirable in a more traditional diplomatic context. Rather, one wants a group marked by mutual respect and trust such that it can tolerate and indeed encourage differences in viewpoints among its members. A person must be able to explore and "try on" a position at variance with his government without eliciting massive social pressure from his fellow countrymen during the workshop. Also he must feel secure that when he returns home he will not be vulnerable to charges that he made unpatriotic statements.

Therefore, because interpersonal openness and group problem-solving activities in the workshop require some level of positive trust among those participants from the same country as well as between participants from different countries, the relations among members from a national group should be closely considered in composing the workshop. If antagonism and distrust exist among members of a national group at the outset of the workshop, then at a minimum the human integration into a total workshop community will take more time. If the divisions—whether based on personality, ethnic membership, social class, or ideology—are so basic as to persist throughout the workshop (as they did in some instances at Fermeda), they will seriously limit the quality and extent of the exploration for innovative solutions.

Thus the ideal of high intragroup trust encourages less

diversity, because each element of diversity increases the likelihood of a barrier to interpersonal trust. Other considerations, however, encourage maximum diversity. For example, one wants a national group with sufficient diversity so that during the workshop it can realistically represent and consider the views of the various forces or factions that exist in its country. Further, in reporting the workshop results, a diverse group will have more credibility with its government and other significant groups in the society. Again there is a problem of achieving an optimum diversity.

In my opinion trust and respect within national groups did not develop to the level where all individual participants who were so inclined could give sustained and vigorous support to a solution that deviated sharply from those that had already been advanced by their own governments. The failure to establish strong national group relations resulted in part from our choice of groupings early in the workshop and in part from self-oriented personal behavior patterns. However, it also resulted from the diversity of the societal forces represented in the national groups, which is the point here.

The tribal tensions in Kenya that followed in the wake of the then recent assassination of Tom Mboya made it especially difficult to create a collaborative team among the Kenyan participants with their different tribal affiliations. Similarly, the deep differences in the political viewpoints among some members of the Ethiopian group limited the quality of trust, if not respect, which they could achieve.

Context

Time

The two-week duration turned out to be inadequate

for the work that had to be done at Fermeda, especially given the workshop composition.

On the one hand, time is required to learn new group patterns of functioning, to develop relations and communications in all of the groupings instrumental to the success of the workshop, to explore areas that are background to the problem, to discuss peripheral and central issues, to be able to disengage from the hard task work and return to it fresh within some pattern of work breaks, to "sleep on" apparently attractive solutions before becoming committed to them, and to disengage from impasses in order to return to them later.

On the other hand, a sense of time pressure can facilitate these activities—of getting acquainted, rationing time to priority background discussion, exploring issues, generating solutions, and converging on areas of agreement. Moreover, excess time not only is wasteful of that valuable human resource, but also can reduce interest and lead to a lower sense of the back-home realities. Thus, again, the question is one of seeking the optimum, given the circumstances.

In the Fermeda workshop it turned out that we were too short on time for at least four important activities: developing relations within the three national groups; developing the total community (General Assembly) into a well-functioning group; "sleeping on" the tentatively proposed solutions by the two working groups before they were considered firm and submitted to the general assembly; retreating from impasses over such matters as the principle of self-determination, in order to break the individual mental sets and the polarized social dynamics and thereby allow for new approaches. We simply had run out of time when these needs became so pressing and apparent. I admit that a different utilization of time in a different design could have allowed for at least the first or second of these developments. In any event, however, in my opinion we did not allow enough time for the third and fourth activities.

To return to the idea that the adequacy of time depends upon workshop composition: if the workshop community is comprised of persons characterized by high intellectual skills, familiarity with the background of the issues, personal openness, and prior positive relations among national group members, then the optimal duration of the workshop is shorter than if these ingredients are not present. To summarize earlier conclusions, some of these factors were favorable and some unfavorable in the Fermeda workshop, and on balance the time was not quite adequate.

As a practical matter it would have been difficult to have lengthened substantially the experimental Fermeda workshop in view of the press of university calendars and personal work responsibilities. In the future, however, if a workshop can be advanced by its sponsors with more confidence in the concept, and if the proposed length is based on a careful analysis of the types of conditions mentioned above, then prospective participants may more readily justify whatever time commitment is requested.

Location

The Fermeda Hotel in the mountains of northern Italy was a favorable choice, satisfactorily meeting many of the requirements for such a venture.

First, since none of the national groups were the home team, there were none of the presumed or actual advantages that accrue from meeting on one's own territory. Moreover, in political terms the Italian location is relatively, if not absolutely, neutral.

Second, it was sufficiently isolated so that there were few, if any, family or professional work distractions. Moreover, the paucity of news on Kenya, Ethiopia, and Somalia in the Italian news media reduced, but did not eliminate the political distractions. News that did get through to Hotel Fermeda included the hijacking of an Ethiopian Airliner by an Eritrean irredentist (an incident that tended to arouse Ethiopian fears about recessionist movements), flare-ups along the Israeli-Arab borders (which have some rough parallels with events in the Horn of Africa), and the allegations of tribal oath taking in Kenya and the developments related to apprehending a Kikiyu charged with the assassination of Mboya, who was a Luo (developments that aroused anxieties within the Kenyan group, which included both Luos and a Kikuyu).

Such comparative insulation from family, work, and political "distractions" allows for a deeper immersion in the mental and emotional processes of the workshop and permits the development of a "cultural island," which in turn encourages participants to challenge cherished assumptions, break old thought processes, and modify attitudes. However, the attitudes, views, and products generated by the workshop must eventually be persuasive also to countrymen who have not attended the workshop; hence it is possible for the cultural-island effect to be too complete if it leads to proposed solutions that will later be dismissed back home as unrealistic or idealistic. Similarly, some would consider the cultural island too complete if upon returning home the participants express conciliatory attitudes sufficiently deviant from the norm of the other influentials to rob them of their credibility.

The implication of these considerations is that, while the more neutral the location the better, there is some optimal degree of insulation from cues reminiscent of the political realities back home. In my opinion Fermeda was close to optimal for a workshop on the border disputes in the Horn of Africa.

Physical Setting

The immediate surroundings of Fermeda played a tactical role in the workshop. The lofty and inspiring mountain views, together with the sunny but brisk weather, reinforced the desired mood; and the mountain paths invited brief after-meal walks that complemented the sedentary workshop meetings. Meals were taken at tables seating four to six generally filled as participants arrived for lunch, a procedure that invariably produced an international mixture. The meals and other aspects of the service were, in my opinion, good to excellent and produced few complaints; this factor may seem trivial to the reader, but in my experience it makes some difference in terms of whether the energy of participants and staff is completely available for the important work of the workshop.

Differentiated Roles

There were no formally differentiated roles among the eighteen African participants. Each had been enlisted directly by the Yale sponsors, and no member of a national group was expected to play any kind of coordinating or leadership role before, during, or after Fermeda. This was an advantage in that it encouraged individual responses and allowed informal leadership to emerge as appropriate to the workshop setting. A possible disadvantage is suggested by the absence of national group mechanisms for dealing with the problems of disruption created by one of their members. While his fellow countrymen evidenced embarrassment and did make some attempts to ameliorate his disruptive actions, neither any individual in his national group nor the group as a whole had any formally sanctioned structure or mechanism for dealing with him; hence the disruption had to be curbed either in the T-group or individually by one of the Yale sponsors. On balance, however, the undifferentiated roles of participants was probably most appropriate in Fermeda. Nevertheless, we would suggest a design in which both preparatory and follow-up activities are considered for a workshop. In that event, there is additional rationale for some formal coordinating role(s) within the national groups.

Other questions pertained to staff roles and observers. What would be the roles during the workshop for the three men from Yale who had sponsored, promoted, and arranged the workshop? How could they relate to the four-man group of trainers?* It was quickly and wisely decided that the sponsoring group would enter into the process as participants during the first week, when our focus would be on the building of relationships and development of sensitivity to group-process issues. We trainers were reluctant to include observers,

---

*The author of this chapter was convinced from the outset that the primary emphasis of the behavioral scientists was to facilitate the process of joint problem solving by the African participants during the workshop rather than personal learning and sensitivity training. For this reason he referred to himself and his three colleagues in the draft of this chapter not as "trainers" but as "process consultants"; and he used the designation "working group" instead of "T-group." The distinction for him involves not semantics but theory. In order to avoid confusion, however, he has agreed to permit me to change his terminology to conform to the rest of the book.—Ed.

because they would tend to be contrary to the fluid participation and deep personal involvement we wanted to promote. It would also have been cruel and inhuman punishment to have excluded the sponsoring group from active involvement even in the early phase of the workshop. Although they reported some personal conflict in being both participants and having special responsibility, they handled the dilemmas well and were very positive forces in the development of the two working groups.

In any event, it was expected that their leadership role would increase as we moved into the substantive discussion. It did, and during the second half of the workshop the roles of the Yale sponsors and the trainers became less and less differentiated, except that the sponsors were more active in the discussion of substantive issues.

The combined staff of sponsors and trainers did agree to invite an interested person to attend part of the workshop. This idea proved unsuccessful because when he arrived a few days before the end of the workshop, he could not appreciate the context in which the events he observed occurred and was not easily included in the little intense society already twelve days old. This result is, in my experience, typical of an attempt to involve observers for a short time during a workshop.

Underlying Purpose and Operational Goal

Whereas the underlying purpose of a workshop is presumably given by the time it must be designed in detail, the specific products or other results to be achieved by the end should be carefully considered. The selection of an appropriate operational goal is a significant element in the design.

The basic substantive purpose for which the Fermeda

workshop was conceived was to contribute to positive solutions that might strengthen peace and security in the Horn of Africa. That purpose was a given; when the Yale group and the trainers met the day before the workshop began, however, to plan roles and activities, the operational goal stated by the Yale sponsors was accepted without challenge or discussion. I now believe that procedure to have been an error, although I did not appreciate it at the time.

The operational goal was to produce a general consensus among participants for some proposal to solve the border dispute. It was presumed that the proposal would be committed to writing, but we were undecided whether it would be released to the press at the end of the conference or would be treated confidentially by individual participants.

As it turned out, the workshop was unable to reach consensus on a proposal. That fact in itself raises the question about the level of the goal—was it too ambitious? Here I want to return to the concept of optimality. The operational goal for a workshop can be set too low (it does not really challenge) or too high (it carries too high a risk of creating a sense of failure).

The goal of a single proposal can be questioned on another basis as well. If it had been achieved, would a single proposal have tended to facilitate or hinder the formal diplomatic negotiations that ultimately would be employed to reach agreement between governments? I believe that it would be more likely to hinder negotiations. There is good chance that one government would be more amenable than another to utilize the workshop's proposal as a point of departure, and the second government might find it advisable to dissociate itself from the workshop, dismissing it as irrelevant. On the other hand, if the workshop's goal had been to. develop two or three proposed solutions, each of which received some international support in the workshop, these documents would have allowed for the flexibility necessary for the formal negotiations between governments.

In any event, the Fermeda experience strengthens my belief that it is desirable for the workshop's immediate goal to be tangible—to produce a document—rather than merely to achieve some level of mutual education and attitude change. Even if the latter are considered the more significant outcomes, they are still better achieved within the disciplining influence of a tangible task. The impressive group work in exploring the primary and secondary issues at Fermeda could have occurred, in my opinion, only under the pressure to produce something specific.

I have lamented that the staff accepted without question the goal of a single proposal. It should be obvious by now that we also failed to make this an explicit issue on the agenda for the total community. Thus we did not test whether in the minds of the participants our operational goal for the workshop was appropriate. At some point I began to appreciate that for many of the participants a single proposal was not an appropriate or salient goal, although these same participants were certainly committed to the underlying purpose of the workshop.

In short, whether or not the specific operational goal toward which the workshop's efforts were organized was appropriate (and I am inclined to believe it was not), it certainly should have been more actively and more explicitly considered by the staff in particular and by the total community in general.

Workshop Activities

The workshop calendar is presented elsewhere; reference to it must be made to gain an appreciation of the chronology of events and a pictorial view of the time allocated to various types of activities. The present discussion will describe the nature and intent of each of various types of workshop activities and evaluate each as an aspect of the overall design. Basically one can conceive the design as comprising the following main elements of activity.

1. Two T-groups
2. Simulations and theory presentations
3. Planning committee
4. General Assembly
5. Free period

T-Groups

The two groups each contained approximately half the population of the community. They were selected so as to contain three participants from each of the three African countries. Two members of the Yale group were in one section, the third was included in the second. Two trainers were assigned to each group. These groups were intentionally unstructured in two important respects. First, the trainers who announced the group assignments and scheduled time for them did not specify any substantive agenda nor any mechanism for deciding upon such an agenda. Second, they did not provide for any chairmanship or other leadership roles for discussions. Instead we stressed that the time allotted to the groups could be used in any way each group chose but that, however they used the time, they were urged to share with each other their own individual reactions and assessments of the group process, in order both to sharpen their skills in diagnosing process and to improve upon the functioning of their respective groups. We also provided illustrations of process analysis and generally facilitated the development of authentic communication and strong positive relations among members.

The lack of a structure (agenda, chairman) to which participants had been accustomed produced early confusion and anger toward the trainers that was not always expressed directly. In these groups—this is typical of similarly unstructured groups—when participants discover that there is no authority to whom they may appeal, the membership issues of rivalry and identity become more salient and are more amenable to resolution or stable accommodation. The groups at Fermeda went through early periods in which any serious initiative by one group member would be blunted or canceled by another member, even if the latter basically concurred with the direction of the former's initiative. When the members of one group acknowledged and attempted to understand this pattern, mutual influence became more prevalent.

As the two-week period progressed and the working groups evolved strong internal relations and effective methods of functioning, they employed their time more and more directly on the substantive problem solving of the border disputes. Each group set its own pace in discussing the issues in dispute.

Simulations, Techniques, and Theory Inputs

On each of the first three days of the workshop a simulation (exercise, game) was used that lasted from an hour and a half to four hours. These experiences illustrated certain theories presented either before or after the simulation. One simulation involved alternate group leadership styles and their effects on group members. The two other simulations structured situations in which participants were presented with the choices of competing or cooperating with other players in striving toward their goals. These experiences allowed the workshop community to explore such ideas as interdependency, reciprocity, perceptions, and expectations. They were designed both to have immediate relevance to the here-and-now processes of managing interpersonal conflict and building collaboration within the two workgroups and to have implications for the subsequent process of problem solving applied to the border disputes. In addition—because they were played in subgroups comprised of at least one Ethiopian, one Somali, and one Kenyan (and usually one American)—they had the intended effect of accelerating the development of interpersonal bonds across national boundaries. Thus during the first few days they were an integral part of the larger strategy of knitting together a human community that could then work effectively on the substantive problems.

Later, on the Sunday beginning the second phase, we introduced the technique of brainstorming and practiced it on solutions to the Nigeria-Biafra war. This exercise was designed to familiarize the total workshop community with the technique so that it could be employed if and when it was deemed useful as a part of our problem-solving activities. It was used subsequently by both working groups, very effectively by one.

In addition to a brief presentation of theory that accompanied the four structured training experiences, we gave two other brief talks about concepts.

In all, the above activities consumed ten to twelve hours over the two-week period. Although the simulations and theory inputs had varied yields, in my opinion the overall contribution at Fermeda was worth the time. In the future this structured material can be even more closely tailored to the composition and purpose of an international problem-solving workshop.

Planning Committee

The two T-groups functioned continuously throughout the workshop until the last day and a half (with changing functions), and the simulations were concentrated in the first several days. In contrast, the planning committee was created late in the first week, when the total workshop community began to focus explicitly on the dispute. The representative planning committee was balanced with respect to T-group and national affiliation. Thus the committee was comprised of two Ethiopians, two Somalis, and two Kenyans; one of the two nationals was drawn from each T-group. These representatives were named in meetings of the national groups. One trainer from each of the two T-groups and one of the Yale representatives were also members of the committee.

During the first five days the trainers had allocated time to such activities as the working groups and had structured some training experiences. They had sought evaluative reactions to each element of the design and had considered these reactions seriously; nevertheless, they had preserved the initiative in decisions involving design. Now a representative committee assumed the authority and responsibility heretofore exercised by the four trainers.

The planning committee appeared to have immediate

legitimacy and functioned effectively as a group. It met at least once a day to review progress and to decide the agenda for work and the groupings within which the work would occur—for example, whether the work would take place in T-groups or at the General Assembly. It opted for a permanent chairman for the planning committee itself but decided to have the General Assembly chaired by participants not on the committee, generally changing the chairmanship for each session, rotating among Somalis, Ethiopians and Kenyans.

Within the concept of the workshop design there are many alternate ways to share control of the workshop. Replacing evaluative feedback and suggestions to the staff with a representative committee is just one strategy. In my opinion the planning committee was an appropriate and effective part of the Fermeda design.

It should be noted that there was one lapse in the implementation of the feedback and consultation mechanism. Our design for the third day of Week 1, when national groups were asked to present views of the other two countries and predict views of their own country, was not adequately tested with participants in advance.

General Assembly

The General Assembly as such was created by the planning committee. On many occasions during the first five days the total community was assembled for a simulation or some presentation, typically followed by open discussion. These meetings of the total community, however, were always auxilliary to other activities or groupings and especially to the working groups. The total community had been a primary place neither for the process of self-government nor for problem-solving discussions.

As a result of the increased focus on substantive issues and in view of the task of creating a single document, the planning committee immediately perceived the need for total community discussions and decision making and consequently created the General Assembly for this purpose.

As it happened, the first chairman of the General Assembly followed parliamentary procedures and, although there were some initial objections, this procedural format persisted.

The General Assembly failed to develop into an effective functioning unit. It started on a note of confusion on the fourth night of the first week and ended on a note of frustration and anger on the final evening. The confusion and frustration were created in part by each of the following: the disruptive actions of one participant; the fact that the Assembly was in a very real sense a new group, with all of the attendent issues of rivalry and identity conflict in the interpersonal relationships across working groups; the existence of some especially important tensions between members of the same national group who had heretofore been in separate working groups; and the abrupt shift from the fluid structure and spontaneity of the working groups to the constraining framework of parliamentary procedure. Resorting to that procedure, I believe, represented partly a method of coping with the first three factors—the disruptive person, the "new group" phenomenon, and tensions among members of the same national group.

Other reasons can be offered to explain why parliamentary procedure was relied upon by the General Assembly. First, it surely is a habitual response to treating the institutional affairs of universities and matters of state, a pattern much more ingrained in the participants than their recently learned pattern of the T-groups. Still the consultants had hoped that the recentness of the experience with the latter would have lead to a more open and flexible procedure in the General Assembly. Second, it is true that as we came closer to making choices about proposed solutions, the stakes became higher, and individuals may have increasingly preferred procedures that were both predictable and impersonal.

One effect of the parliamentary procedure was seriously to circumscribe the effectiveness of the trainees as long as they abided by the same rules. Unfortunately we did not make an issue of the constraint; if we had, we might well have been legitimately exempted, since we were not making substantive contributions. A special privilege to intervene in connection with the process of interaction might have seemed reasonable.

Because the initial and second experiences with the General Assembly were discouraging, the planning committee, reflecting the general sentiment of the community, placed heavy reliance upon the T-groups to carry on the substantive problem solving. Thus little use was made of the General Assembly until the last working day. We were still pressing to come up with a general consensus on a single proposed solution and therefore the General Assembly became the primary and exclusive vehicle for the debate, integration, compromise, and agreement we sought. The method did not work.

Breaks in the Work Routine

The schedule was heavy, with working sessions during the morning, afternoon, and evening. During the first week there was typically a break from about 4:00 P.M. to 8:00 P.M., allowing for recreation and socializing as well as a relaxed dinner. The break was shorter during the second week as a result of the press of work. We had planned a two-day break in the middle of the workshop, allowing for people to regenerate for the second week. In my opinion the Fermeda work schedule was about right.

Groupings

Although some of the ideas were implicit in my earlier discussion of activities and membership composition, I want to give explicit treatment to the importance of the groupings emphasized at Fermeda.

The initial grouping emphasized was the split-half of the workshop. It was in these T-groups that we worked on managing the issues of rivalry, membership, and trust; and it was within these groups that we developed authentic communication, strong relationships, and effective patterns of mutual influence. These groups served well the purposes of the workshop—as far as they could take them. The problem was that they did not enable us to approach the operational goal.

In contrast, two groupings that turned out to be important but to which we did not give any early emphasis were the national groups and the total community. The first presented a problem I had anticipated at the outset; I had therefore argued for a design in which each of three trainers would work with one of the three national groups before we placed much emphasis on the development of groupings with multinational composition, such as the working groups. Some of my reasoning about the importance of trusting relations within national groups is presented in my discussion of the composition of participants recruited. In the case of Fermeda we had not recruited persons who already had close relationships with each other. Their perceptions and attitudes toward each other were unknowns. Their informal social hierarchy was an unknown. I thought it would be wise, therefore, for us to work with each national group alone at the outset and then periodically throughout the workshop. This method would have enabled us to appreciate the strains, if any, that were there and to facilitate the resolution or management of these tensions.

The counterargument, which prevailed among the trainers, was one based on the principle of primacy: we should give early emphasis to the establishment of interpersonal relationships that cross country boundaries because they were expected to be the most difficult to establish and the most directly instrumental to solving the problem of the dispute. It was feared that by reinforcing national identification and groupings early in the workshop, we would risk increasing in-group solidarity and making interpersonal relationships across national groups more difficult to attain.

Unfortunately, because of the unavoidable but horrible inadequacy of planning time (one day in Rome), we could not fully explore this design issue or consider the key assumptions and so weigh the pros and cons. We had to move on to the other design and to logistic questions without consensus on this important one.

When the design finally did provide for work within the three national groups on the fifth day, the trainer found the participants reluctant to work in these groups. Although the reluctance we encountered was strengthened by some resistance to the specific task for which they were to caucus in national groups, the rifts within groups that soon became evident confirmed that there were avoidance tendencies based on a lack of trust, especially strong in the Kenyan group and moderately strong among the Ethiopians.

At this point the initiative and final say over the work-shop design had been transferred to the representative planning committee. The trainers' suggestion that some diagnosis and problem-solving work occur within periodic meetings of national groups and that a consultant meet with each of these groups was not accepted.

On the last two days there were private ad hoc caucuses by national groups (containing either a majority or all of the members), but we know little of the nature of these meetings except that there were sharp differences and some instances of strong attempts to exert influence among fellow nationals.

Had we built national groups into the design at a very early stage and attached trainees to these groups we would have been accepted, albeit perhaps with resistance. In any event, the sources of resistance could have been explored within the groups, and the importance of intranational group trust could have been underscored and facilitated. In my opinion, better relations within national groups could have made a significant difference at Fermeda by improving the quality of the deliberations during the last two days and by increasing the chance of the community's converging on some areas of substantive agreement.

As mentioned earlier, we also failed to build an effective group out of the total community. The community was comprised of twenty-five persons; while that is a large group it was still quite possible to create a flexible open social unit with many of the same characteristics of the two working groups. We did not become acutely aware of the crucial need to develop that social unit until we were already into the substantive discussions and until our control had been transferred to the planning committee; consequently, we had less leverage on the design. By that time the T-groups also seemed so much more promising for useful problem solving that no one was really prepared to argue strongly that we forego the immediate progress those groups could achieve. We did not really have good options at that point.

It may be useful here to underscore the interrelationship between two key aspects of the workshop. The goal of achieving a single solution had an important relationship to the type of groupings we needed to develop during the workshop. If we did not have this particular goal, the General Assembly probably would not have deserved any more attention than we gave it. But with this goal we should have worked seriously on the development of valid communication and trust in the total community just as soon as the working groups had crystallized, if not sooner. I believe our oversight regarding the General Assembly was due to our failure to think through the implications of the goal as well as our failure to appreciate the strains within national groups.

Workshop as a Singular Event

A major question is whether or not a particular workshop is conceived as a part of a larger project. Fermeda was more or less a single event, with no systematic preparatory activities for participants nor any planned follow-up activities. We have entertained ideas for different formal follow-up efforts, and I hope some occur. For this first effort the magnitude of the achievement of arranging participation in and support for the actual workshop itself would have discouraged normal men. No one could have expected more.

In future workshop projects serious thought should be given to preparatory team building within national groups (of the prospective participants) as well as to background preparation. These groups formed in advance of the workshop could be consulted about some aspects of the design, including the operational goals for the workshop itself. It might well turn out that it would be appropriate to have, for example, two-week workshop in neutral territory followed by two sessions of five days each, the first held in one of the participating countries and the second in another.

The design might possibly involve the introduction of additional participants during these second two sessions either because of their particular expertise or because of their relationship to the governments (or opposition forces) in the countries.

These are only a few of the design possibilities for a larger project and are supplied here merely as suggestions. I hope these and other possibilities are tested in our search for better methods for solving international problems and avoiding wars. Whether they are given a chance depends upon whether other scholars, bureaucrats, and men of affairs will follow the lead of the high-minded and stubborn Yale professors who brought the Fermeda workshop to fruition. These promoters are the scare resource. There is a ready supply of trainers like me and my three colleagues, who stand in the wings ready to make our particular contribution.

9. Toward a Solution?

By Leonard W. Doob, William J. Foltz, and Robert B. Stevens

When the idea of Fermeda was originally conceived, we had hoped that the participants themselves would arrive at a joint solution, embrace it enthusiastically, carry it home to their respective foreign offices, and then—the fantasy luckily halted at this point. In fact, the reader now knows, no unanimity was reached. But we feel that the two T-groups' deliberations did suggest, if not the perfect instant solution, at least a path toward a solution that the three governments might find preferable to their present armed suspicions. In this chapter the three of us speak entirely for ourselves in presenting our vision of where such a path may lie.

We hasten to add that, while the participants provided the inspiration and many of the ideas, they have no individual or group responsibility for ways in which we have interpreted and organized their thoughts—but we are grateful to them. What we present here is an unsolicited act of power brokering, although we are acutely aware that the world has relegated academic persons like us to what used to be thought of as an ivory tower. Without Fermeda we might have been able to concoct from books, experience, and imagination a more brilliant plan from the standpoint of our academic colleagues, but as a result of Fermeda we think that we have a proposal more likely to appear promising to policy makers in the three African countries.

Stumbling Blocks

The Somali border disputes involve a clash between the

immovable object, representing the unwillingness of the Somali government to discuss the problem in terms other than ultimate self-determination, and the irresistible force, representing the unwillingness of the Kenya and Ethiopian governments to think and talk in terms other than those based on the preservation of existing political boundaries. We know that these views represent more than official platitudes. In each case a strong and widespread sense of national identity and pride in that identity underlies them. The identity and pride exist regardless of an individual's feelings about the current political regime in his country or about the other ethnic groups of his nation. National symbolism is a potent force that could be neither denied nor countered during our discussion at Fermeda.

At the same time few politically important persons in Kenya and Ethiopia seem to have been directly injured by the continuation of the border disputes; and the same is true, if to a lesser degree, of their Somali counterparts. It is unlikely, therefore, that the leaders will make major sacrifices of other deeply cherished values to settle the conflict, particularly since no instant and overwhelmingly important political reward will probably be accorded the peace makers. On the other hand, if a solution were devised that in form or substance does not undermine these values, assent could perhaps be obtained.

From our standpoint, the first stumbling block to a solution of the disputes is the emotional commitment to the abstract concepts of self-determination and national sovereignty. If ever one regrets the influence of European history and practice on African thought, it is indeed in connection with the reification of these doctrines, products themselves of European nineteenth-century politics and exported to the Horn of East Africa as part of Europe's futile attempt to resolve its contradictions at the expense of others. "Self-determination" in Africa raises the same problems of delimitation and restraint as it does in Ulster, Gibraltar, Brittany, and Georgia. Much of the conflict existing on the Kenya-Somalia border was produced by Britain's inept and half-hearted use of theories of self-determination in the 1950s. So it is with "sovereignty," a notion increasingly regarded as pedantic and formalistic in those countries that exported it to Africa.

Both sovereignty and self-determination were important ideological and psychological weapons in Africa's political struggle for freedom from European rule, and it is certainly understandable that these concepts should have a ring of authority and importance in the Horn. Yet the commitment to these symbolic representations of independence—as if they represented a pure objective standard—undermines most possibilities for settlement of that strife-torn area. Fermeda provided ample evidence that this commitment was not an empty one, in which the exalted concepts were trotted out to help score debating points; rather, the pattern was seemingly one of the words' inner logic driving a man to defend "our people" or "our national dignity" with even more passion than would otherwise be mounted. This logic, however, can by itself produce little reconciliation in the real world; and some form of peaceful coexistence, such as that between the OAU Charter's enshrinement of national boundaries and the UN Charter's pledge of self-determination, is probably the best that can be hoped for.

The conflicting rhetoric of sovereignty and self-determination coexists uneasily with the equally powerful rhetoric of a second stumbling block. "Unity" is a concept that African nationals—just like their counterparts in other areas of the world—use extensively in trying to influence and resolve problems with one another. While the rhetoric of unity is more qualified than it was, say, five years ago, African unity is an ultimate goal that appeals as much to African intellectuals as it does to African politicians.

This feeling is deeply rooted—for excellent reasons—in the experience of those who have grown up or built their careers during the nationalist struggle against European rule, but at the present moment in history it seems unlikely to have the direct applicability to international affairs that it has had to domestic political life. In East Africa today the facile enthusiasm for continent-wide unity has largely given way to a somewhat more limited emphasis on regionalism. As applied to the Horn, "regionalism" has come to mean admission to the East African Community. This organization in and of itself is of great potential utility in many domains of economic and political life, but it is important to appreciate the present fragility of the Community and the limits of the political benefits that increased membership would provide. While the East African Community could be the basis of a federal state, it is very much not that at the moment. It is a loose form of common market, coupled with limited common services. Some of the institutions of a federal state are available, although they can be used only with respect to relatively narrow issues. While we commend the idea of the Community and of the adhesion of other countries, we are convinced that it would be misleading to contend that the Community in its present state is the equivalent of political union. For this reason we are skeptical of the assumption that, if

Somalia and Ethiopia join the Community, the border disputes will somehow evaporate.

Even if Kenya and Ethiopia could soften their insistence upon the inalienable sovereignty and adopt a more realistic view of formal African unity and regionalism, they would probably cling to their conviction that, in return for whatever concessions they might be prepared to make, Somalia has nothing to offer in return. This situation presents a third stumbling block. Perhaps a symbolic act might be sufficient, but it well might be argued that the Somalis do have a number of real resources they could surrender in return for changes in the status of the disputed areas.

A fourth block, more psychological than real, is the pervasive fear each country has of the other's military power. It is as if each side recognizes its own military weakness but does not attribute this to the state of military ineffectiveness in the region as a whole. From a military point of view, none of the three states is in a position to mount successfully any sort of sustained attack on a substantial portion of another's territory, nor, given the natural advantages accruing to the defense, is it likely soon to acquire such capability. Unfortunately the disastrous great-power myths of the needs for "arms parity" and even "military superiority," with their accompanying fears of "weapons gaps," have been almost as potent in the Horn as in Washington and Moscow. Despite the mini-arms race, neither the Somali nor the Kenyan army has the logistic capacity to venture in force far from its borders, and the Ethiopian army, marginally better endowed with equipment and much larger in numbers that its neighbors, appears to have all it can do to handle the Empire's other trouble spots.

Levels

Short of conquering the three countries and forcing them to resolve their disputes—a procedure we definitely do not recommend—we feel that no immediate or acceptable solution is likely to be achieved in the Horn. Diminishing the feelings concerning sovereignty, continental or regional symbolism, a quid pro quo, or military might cannot be attained by a classic confrontation. Instead the three countries and their leaders must learn by doing, and doing here means working together on step-by-step solutions. The experience gained from one bit of cooperation, it is hoped, could enable the participants to ascend to a still higher level. Very broadly we think that the ideal evolution would be through a series of progressive solution stages, each of which could be an acceptable "final" stage if further progress proved impossible but each of which would set in play various forces pushing for greater stability and security as well as permitting the achievement of other highly ranked goals. Such a graded solution might begin by solemnizing the current detente, rise through a series of enforceable commitments to the OAU and the EAC, and finally end in a serious compromise involving all parties in gains and losses.

Throughout this development from level to level it is essential that no step violate the high domestic priorities of each country. This is especially important for Kenya and Ethiopia, for whom the border issue is of lesser salience. Important and relevant domestic priorities for Kenya, likely to continue under any regime, are economic development with industrialization, and maintenance of some ethnic balance within the regime. For Ethiopia, the most relevant continuing domestic priority is probably the retention of Eritrea, although that priority may be shifting toward the kind of development that now characterizes Kenya. As suggested earlier, the border dispute itself has been a more significant policy issue in Somalia, but even here the other priorities of a developing nation must not be ignored entirely in producing acceptable solutions.

Joint Administration Area

The first level, largely negative, has already been attained. Just continuing the present uneasy detente is a form of solving the killing and social disruption that previously existed. The next level is a further implementation of the detente: a transitional period of military neutralization of the Ogaden and North Eastern Province, with parallel Somali military pullbacks from the borders and with a guarantee of free movement of people and animals across the borders. This agreement would help to diminish anxiety from military sources and would be a concrete and meaningful token of international cooperation. At this point the territorial status quo is merely reaffirmed but on a more solid and less threatening basis.

The proposal to whittle away the notion of absolute sovereignty and to establish a fruitful if limited form of cooperation involves the establishment of a Joint Administration Area (JAA) for the areas under dispute. The precise form and substance of this organization must depend upon the degree to which the three countries will make some sacrifices in order to achieve a solution. Certain minimum commitments, however, seem essential. For the Area at least, the three countries would agree that the question of ultimate sovereignty be "put in the freezer" without prejudice to anyone's ultimate case during the existence of the JAA. A series of governmental decisions must then be made. Persons determined to be inhabitants of the area for at least six months of the year will be issued documents in the name of the JAA and of the three countries. At the same time free movement will be guaranteed in and out of the JAA. For those citizens of the three countries not holding JAA documents, the movement may be restricted in ways to be agreed upon.

The administration of the JAA should draw as much as possible on the human resources of the people of the area. Other persons should be recruited according to a quota system. The language of the administration should be that of the people of the area—Somali, with English used for written communication. Customary courts should be used for dispute settlement and most other cases wherever possible, with a single court of appeals set up by the JAA. International taxation should be based on livestock sales only, with the JAA receiving additional tax funds from an appropriate rebate from import duties collected at the port of entry by the three countries. The school system will at least initially be confined to the primary level under the authority of the JAA. Somali will be the system's language, with English instruction begun as early as feasible. Muslim schools will continue to exist.

If any mineral were found anywhere in the JAA (and we are well aware that such a find could aggravate the dispute considerably), the royalties would be divided four ways: 25 per cent to each of the three countries establishing the JAA, and the fourth quarter to the Administration itself. Internal order would be assured by a constabulary under the orders of the JAA administration. This force might initially include a substantial number of men detached from units now serving in the three countries. Since police officers must be competent in the local language, most of them will be ethnically Somalis. The military neutrality of the area and its strict demilitarization will have to be embodied in the treaty setting up the JAA.

When the JAA is established, outside funding would be required from the three establishing states and through international bodies. Any development should emphasize settlement of the nomadic population—an objective in accord with the existing plans of all three countries. Plans involving major developments will have to be financed heavily from outside, ideally through loans guaranteed jointly by each of the three nations. The plans should be harmonized with relevant activities of the East African Community. Disputes among the three countries, or between the JAA and any or all of the three countries, should be arbitrated by a standing panel under the auspices of the Organization of African Unity, the EAC, or some similar outside body.

It is not difficult to describe the general form the JAA should take, and the three countries certainly possess enough resourceful technicians to hammer out the myriad details. As suggested earlier, the major stumbling block is related to the issue of sovereignty. To proceed, then: the JAA would remain legally a condominium, each of the three states having the right to reclaim the territory ceded to it should there be a breach of the treaty that established the state. Such right, however, could not be judged subjectively and unilaterally but would have to be settled by an arbitration tribunal whose balanced membership and chairmanship from outside the area would be carefully spelled out in the treaty.

So far in this exposition we have veered away from the stumbling block that must be overcome if Kenya and Ethiopia are to join the JAA, the quid pro quo they demand from Somalia. The disputed areas, of course, are not in Somalia, and Kenya and Ethiopia understandably take the position that Somalia is interested solely in gaining land without making some sort of contribution. This theme was often reiterated at Fermeda, and some of the participants even suggested that Somalia has nothing to contribute. The Somalis, in turn, have a very strong case to the effect that they should not be obliged to give up any territory, since none of their land is in dispute. We would argue, then, that a formula should be devised by which Somalia would be required to give up territory and would be seen to be making a substantial material contribution. We propose agreement on a flexible formula whereby the ultimate size of the JAA would be determined by the amount of land that Somalia would cede. Such a formula might be that for every square mile of Somali territory included in the JAA, the other countries would yield two square miles each. Thus Somalia would be required to contribute a significant amount of its homeland in order to produce a greater Somalia, even if that greater Somalia were still partly controlled by Kenya and Ethiopia, albeit having considerable local autonomy.

Thereafter

From the JAA, and the experience it could provide over the years, two consequences, we hope, might flow, perhaps even as a result of the administrative complexities of that organization. First, the leaders of the state would discover that they could work together in settling the disputes. They themselves will have evolved and de-

vised new forms of cooperation, new kinds of mechanisms that they—and certainly we—cannot anticipate at
the outset of the enterprise. Theirs would be the decision concerning the precise details of the thereafter—
though, it should be noted, the inertial energy built up
by a successful administering authority should provide
bureaucratic pressures for continued, indeed expanded,
cooperation. Then the three nations certainly will have
learned that as states they can survive even without
exercising complete sovereignty over areas they now
consider theirs for historical, ethnic, legal, or moral reasons. Under such circumstances it is conceivable that the
issue of sovereignty could become less salient. Perhaps
even the present objections voiced by Kenya and Ethiopia to a popular plebiscite might be removed. It seems
unlikely that such a plebiscite would result in anything
other than a desire for integration into the Somali state.
But whether or not there were in fact such a decision, it
might be possible to allow a de facto and de jure absorb-
ing by Somalia of the JAA, provided—again the stumbling block—Somalia could then again offer Kenya and
Ethiopia a significant quid pro quo.

Somalia could, of course, guarantee Ethiopia its support for the maintenance of Ethiopia's other borders.
This agreement could be embodied in a mutual-defense
treaty and would have the effect of putting Somalia in
the position of defending Ethiopia before the various
Muslim nations who want to split off Eritrea. Thus, instead of beginning the dismemberment of the Ethiopian
empire, the cession of the Ogaden could have the effect
of strengthening the Empire. Further, in the likely event
that post-Gaullist France will some day decide it has no
further interest in retaining control over the French Territory of the Afar and the Issa, with Djibuti as its
strategic port and railroad terminus, the Somalis can

guarantee a peaceful settlement, giving Ethiopia, at the minimum control over its one vital railroad link with the seas and free access to the port. No doubt promise of such a peaceful agreement would hasten France's decision to leave its last African colony.

For the Kenyans, the Somalis could offer to accept technically unfavorable conditions for association with the East African Community. While we have expressed skepticism about the more extravagant political claims made for joining the East African Community, Somalia could be admitted on economic terms designed to be unusually attractive to Kenya. At the moment, as participants at Fermeda reminded one another, Somalia is anxious to join the East African Community—and particularly the common market part of it—on terms that would be very favorable to Somalia's development plans. The members of the Community are now allowed under certain circumstances to protect infant industries through two devices—a transfer tax and a system of quantitative restrictions. A modified measure of industrial licensing is employed. Industries may also be developed specifically through quota manipulations in the East African Development Bank. We would suggest that Somalia, instead of receiving the economically advantageous terms it ordinarily might seek, would be admitted with no protection for industrial growth.

An arrangement which gave Somalia no right to impose quantitative restrictions nor a transfer tax, and which restricted its rights in the Development Bank, would have the result that Somalia would remain economically a pastoral and agricultural society. With an external tariff common to the whole community and assuming improved communications, Somalia would rapidly become economically heavily dependent on Kenya (and to a lesser extent on Ethiopia) for locally manufactured goods. Somalia would supply them (and others) with food products and raw materials, but it would abandon whatever small hope it currently has of developing a modern manufacturing base. Perhaps Kenya would be prepared to reconsider the sovereignty problem in return for such an economic arrangement.

The overall effect of the entire development would be that, perhaps in ten years' time, directly or indirectly Somalia would have achieved its goal of a greater Somalia. Ethiopia and Kenya would have suffered an important blow; their sacrosanct borders would have been violated. But their other borders would have been guaranteed by Somalia and internationally. The new greater Somalia would provide a noncompeting, guaranteed market for its industrializing neighbors. Once again, this result could be embodied in a treaty with the appropriate international guarantees and adjudication.

We would end this proposal with a word of realistic caution. We have kept constantly with us the thought that no proposal can be of any utility if the people who actually exercise power do not want to resolve the conflict. Whether they resolve it—and if so, how—are—indeed, must be—decisions for them and their countrymen. We hope the speculations in this chapter may serve as a goad and an opportunity to show presumptuous outsiders that other approaches designed by Africans themselves will produce a better settlement. Should some rare combination of events lead the appropriate men to take guidance from any of the ideas generated by the Fermeda workshop, they, more closely than we, will have to live with the results. Ultimately, too, the border disputes can be resolved only by the people of the Horn.

Appendix 1. The Consent of the Participants and of Governments

by Leonard W. Doob

The description of our tribulations in each country follows a chronological sequence, beginning with my visit in 1966.

Ethiopia

Before leaving America, I was advised by an American who had held a high position in the university at Addis Ababa that my only chance of succeeding lay in going as high as possible in the university to secure permission and to obtain very influential scholars. The president of the university, a very important Ethiopian, was not available; contact was therefore established with the academic vice-president who, being an American and having just arrived at his post, could provide only mild encouragement and the names of various academic officials. Eventually six people were seen at least once, and they enthusiastically agreed to attend if invited and if they had the time. One man refused on the grounds that a workshop would accomplish very little or nothing either from a political or from a research standpoint; but he claimed that he would attend without consulting the government if he were so inclined.

The interested ones, however, insisted that the government's permission be obtained because they might otherwise not be granted passports, and they could not afford to jeopardize their academic careers. They and others used the phrase "academic freedom" again and again, sometimes by asserting that the university enjoyed such freedom, sometimes by claiming that at this stage of the country's development complete freedom was neither possible nor desirable. The idea seemed to be that, although academic persons have the right to attend an international conference, somehow this workshop would involve Ethiopian prestige as a result of the presence of the Somalis; if the Ethiopians were permitted to attend, one high official said, it was presumed that they would not express "un-Ethiopian ideas" upon their return.

It was not at all easy for me as a private person to approach "the Ethiopian government." Through the helpful offices of some of the academic people, I eventually saw the legal adviser to the Prime Minister, the legal adviser to the Minister of Foreign Affairs, and then the Foreign Minister himself. They agreed that a confrontation with the Somalis would be desirable, but that the Somalis would have to make concessions, since the Ethiopian cause is just and nonnegotiable. No decision, however, could be reached during my stay in Ethiopia: the president of the university and the Emperor were touring the provinces, and no meeting with them could be arranged. Just before leaving for Kenya, however, I was told that the decision would be communicated to me through the Ethiopian ambassador in Nairobi or that through him I would hear whether I should return to Addis to see the president or, possibly, the Emperor.

No word ever came to me in Kenya, though I plagued the switchboard of the Ethiopian embassy. Through intermediaries I learned after my return to Yale that the project had probably been described to the Emperor and that his decision eventually would depend on whether the timing of the workshop appeared propitious from the standpoint of his country's best interest.

Exactly three months later the president of the university wrote me that the men "will not be able to participate in your proposed research" since "the University is
under considerable pressure of work."

Foltz and Stevens encountered no official difficulties
when they visited Addis Ababa in 1968, nor did I in
1969. For by then, as I have explained in Chapter 1,
government had voiced no objection to the enterprise. A
vice-president of the University was enthusiastic about
the project and explained to them that the decision was
now solely within the jurisdiction of his institution. In
1969 the man who had then become president of the
university was the first person I had invited to attend
the workshop in 1966; he himself was too busy to
accept our invitation a third time, but he permitted me
to tell potential participants that the project had academic support. One Ethiopian scholar whom we were
especially anxious to include at first was furious when I
visited him again, because twice before he had re-
arranged his plans at great personal inconvenience; he
understood, of course, that the responsibility for the
postponements was not ours; but alas, this time he
could not come and instead recommended a very competent substitute.

Kenya

Again the first contact was attempted with the highest
official of the university then in Nairobi, the deputy
principal. While awaiting a conference with him, I was
able to see a number of scholars I knew or who had
been recommended to me. In comparison with their
counterparts in Ethiopia and later in Somalia, they
seemed only mildly interested in the conflict on the

border of their country: the North Eastern Province, from their standpoint, is a remote area and presents no very pressing problem. It was possible, then, to secure the lukewarm assent of six very well-qualified persons. Again one man refused: an American, he said, should not try to interfere in African affairs.

Many of the potential participants, and also the deputy principal when he finally consented to see me, laid down two conditions. First, the Kenyan government had to be informed. Again it was no easy task to inform a government, for there was no agreement as to which division should be informed; for example, was the matter of greater concern to the Foreign Office than to the Ministry of Defense? No one, whether African or European, moreover, was eager to arrange an appointment for me; and the secretaries to permanent secretaries of the relevant ministries seemed to have as their principal function the protection of their chiefs against visitors, especially an American. Two permanent secretaries in the relevant ministries flatly refused to see me. Finally, therefore, I visited an African acquaintance, a very capable man holding a high position in Kenyan journalism. In minutes he was able to speak with the Attorney General—by long-distance telephone, because President Kenyatta at the time was vacationing at Mombasa—who asked me to telephone him directly. Without difficulty I reached him and briefly explained the project. That evening as he indicated to the journalist the following day, he spoke with Mr. Kenyatta, who apparently had no objection to the scheme. Thus government was informed but, alas, a misunderstanding arose at this point: the Attorney General somehow felt that the workshop was about to occur and hence suggested that the men at the university telephone his office to verify the government's attitude. How, then, could this consent be preserved for some point in the indefinite future? I wrote a long letter to the Attorney General, outlining the project and summarizing our conversations; this, it was hoped, would constitute the "record" in his office to which reference in the future could be made.

The second requirement of the scholars and of the deputy principal was that a few men from the two other East African universities be asked to participate, because in theory—but less so in practice as time goes on—all three institutions are part of the same university system. Foltz, then in Uganda, invited a political scientist; making a quick trip to Tanzania, I located two political scientists and a historian, all of whom accepted with enthusiasm and alacrity; the vice-principals of both institutions gave their consent, and one offered his campus as a site for the meeting, though timing considerations eventually ruled this out. The governments' permission was not considered necessary: the countries are not directly involved in the disputes and have only a friendly interest in seeing them settled.

I subsequently discovered that some of our Somali participants objected to the idea of persons from Uganda and Tanzania attending for they assumed that the Kenyan case, as it were, would thus be numerically strengthened. In our subsequent visits to Nairobi the issue was raised again by only one of the Kenyans, and therefore we simply never reissued the invitations. The exception, an important Kenyan scholar, found it impossible to accept our third invitation, and when I told him that no other East Africans would be present, he launched an attack on the Somalis for having raised the objection and concluded, with great hostility, that obviously the project itself was "premature," since the Somalis were not thinking in broad East African terms.

It was in Nairobi during the last trip that I made a significant dreadful mistake which still haunts me: I invited one person whose aberrant behavior during the workshop, as noted in various chapters of this book, proved repeatedly disruptive. I consider the reasons for the error of more than passing interest. First, I was introduced to the man when I was having difficulty finding competent persons who were able and willing to attend; the two previous cancellations of the workshop had diminished confidence in us. Nairobi was my last stop; because the workshop was to begin in less than a month, I was anxious to fill our quota of six participants (in fact, I never did; Stevens on another mission a week later had to find a substitute for one individual who in the interim had to decline); I was dreadfully weary; and then, right in the middle of recruiting the Kenyans, Tom Mboya was assassinated. I quickly discovered that this individual had a reputation in the university community of being obstinate and difficult, but I decided to overlook this fact. He came from a tribe I thought should be represented in the Kenyan group; he expressed keen interest and gave the impression of having previously been through a somewhat similar experience in a European country; and I was attracted by his enthusiastic manner of expression. His reputation I dismissed as a function of his cultural background, and I had confidence that the trainers and we could cope with him. But I was wrong, dreadfully wrong: his numerous pathologies and philosophy, in my opinion, turned out to be not cultural but idiosyncratic.

Somalia

Since Somalia had no university at the time, another route to participants had to be employed. Fortunately I had no difficulty establishing contacts in Mogadiscio, the capital: I had spent part of the previous summer in Somalia, was known by important officials, and had the active support of a very influential and understanding individual. I decided, therefore, to invite persons who had studied abroad and who were in strategic positions, if possible connected with research, either in the community or in divisions of government not directly concerned with foreign policy. All the Somalis I approached eagerly responded; whatever hesitation they exhibited clearly stemmed from uncertainty as to whether they could afford the time away from their regular jobs. Even before I left Somalia, as so often happens with elite in Africa, one man's position was shifted abroad, so that he might not be able to attend. Cooperation from Somali officials was complete, I discovered as I conferred informally with the Minister of Foreign Affairs and with the Prime Minister. Permission for government employees to leave the country and to be on leave, with full pay, during the workshop was quickly granted. Only in Somalia did I visit the American embassy, and then for reasons not connected with workshop.

During our two subsequent trips to Somalia, moreover, members of the Embassy were very kind and helpful in arranging appointments and mechanical details, but they played no role whatsoever in the selection of the participants. The delay in the workshop gave rise to fewer changes in personnel in Somalia than in either of the other two countries, in part because the absence of a university made personal schedules more flexible, and

perhaps also because the Somalis have the greater interest in the border disputes.

The new prime minister with whom Foltz discussed
the project in January 1968 stated that he had no objection to the workshop but wondered whether scholars
from one of the other countries would express themselves as freely as the Somali participants. This was the
same man who a few months later caused us to postpone the workshop for another year. When I saw him in
June 1969, aside from seeking that "green light," I emphasized that the selection of participants would have to
be ours and not his and that his government would
therefore have no responsibility for the workshop. I also
petitioned him to grant leaves with pay to the government employees among our participants. He agreed gra-
ciously to both requests.

Appendix 2. Recent History of Workshops in Africa

by Thomas A. Wickes

Chapter 2 contains an account of the original series of workshops underwritten by the Ford Foundation, by various local and national governments, and by other African organizations. That account brings the story up to 1964. At that time new efforts began developing in Coastal East and West Africa and in North Africa; these had varied foci, sponsors, and participants and met with varying degrees of success. Many of the American trainers who had presented the 1961-64 series went to other places in Africa and continued to use laboratory training as part of their work.

From August 30 to October 16, 1965, the Danish Board for Technical Cooperation with Developing Countries, Swedish authorities, and the Ford Foundation co-sponsored a seminar on "The Development and Organization of Vocational Training and Technical Education" (VTTE). This effort brought together twenty-four participants from the East Africa Common Services Organization (administrative civil service body serving Uganda, Kenya, and Tanzania), the United Arab Republic, Uganda, Tunisia, Tanzania, Nigeria, Syria, Saudi Arabia, Lebanon, Jordan, and Iraq.[1]

The seminar was held in Denmark at the Hørsholm High School and was designed to encourage the participants to examine .the view that these developing countries needed a comprehensive vocational training and technical education system as a prerequisite for economic and industrial growth. They were given an opportunity to study existing systems and to develop philosophies and approaches they thought might fit their own

unique situation. Attempts were also made to strength-
en and/or develop their diagnostic, planning, and deci-
sion-making skills.

The seminar started with a brief introduction dealing
with social and cultural change as it was happening in
the Scandinavian setting and as it might apply to the
participants' own education/training efforts back home.
This brief introduction was followed by an eight-day
human-relations workshop or sensitivity-training lab.
The rationale for preceding the greater part of the program with a laboratory experience was straightforward.
The sponsors and staff members recognized that participants came from diverse cultures and had diverse experi-
ential and educational backgrounds. It was important
for them to see each other as nonthreatening sources of
information, to whom each could turn when diagnosing
his own local situations and needs and in designing programs that could be usefully and effectively implemented back home. The participants did talk about many of
the problems they faced back home in getting their own
vocational and technical education systems underway.
For example, in many of their countries vocation-
al/technical school educations were seen as distinctly
inferior to other kinds. Clerks often considered themselves socially "better" than engineers or electronics
technicians because they were performing gentlemen's
work and did not get dirty hands. Part of what was
worked on was implementation problems. The participants knew it would be one thing to get enough technical data about VTTE systems to start one at home and
quite another to overcome all the resistances that would
stand in the way of a successful program both within
and outside their educational structures.

Comments on questionnaires at the end of the seminar

and comments from some of the staff members[2] indicate that the laboratory section of the seminar was well received and thought to be of value by most of the participants. A number, however, saw the laboratory as insignificant or childish or irrelevant.

Here, as in the Fermeda experience, the staff was left with the idea that the laboratory did materially help to open the participants to learning and did markedly reduce the number of interpersonal "games" people tend to play in conferences attended by participants who do not know each other and who have different aims and goals at the outset. Though the evidence was not starkly decisive, the staff was sufficiently encouraged to recommend the laboratory section of the program for use in similar international efforts.

There was very little similarity between the task set for the VTTE seminar and that undertaken at Fermeda. Most immediately noticeable are the emotion-arousing properties of the task itself. The VTTE participants were focused on tasks not nearly as close to raw emotion as are the boundaries of nations. Yet, clearly, people from several African cultures saw the laboratory experience as helpful in the VTTE setting, especially in terms of gaining greater understanding of each other as people. Thus there is strong reason to believe that the method can also facilitate talking about border issues and similar tasks.

From 1964 through 1967 several series of laboratory applications were under way at the same time, though they were not held in conjunction with each other. Perhaps the most extensive applications were in East Africa (Kenya, Zambia, Uganda, Tanzania). Better than a dozen workshops of varying kinds and applications took place there, usually under the joint auspices of the Ford Foundation and other specific national organizations, such as the Kenya Israeli School of Social Work, the Kenya Institute of Administration, the Zambia Civil Service, etc. Most of these lasted one week, though some went on for two. The major designers and staffers of these labs were J. Anthony Stout[3] and Donald Nylen.[4] Nylen was then one of the Ford Foundation's roving education-training consultants, and his beat was primarily Africa. Stout worked for the Ford Foundation, first with the Uganda Electricity Board and later with the Foundation's office in Nairobi. Both of them also helped staff the 1961-64 lab series.

Nylen was the most instrumental in developing and guiding the labs. In fact, in the wording of some Nigerians, he can be called the Baba or Father of Laboratory Training in Africa. He first went to Africa for the Ford Foundation in 1958. As an experienced trainer he began to see and talk with the Foundation about what possibilities human relations training (as he called it) offered to the training efforts of underdeveloped countries. It was he, along with Robert Mitchell (currently with the International Institute of Tropical Agriculture, Ibadan, Nigeria), who organized what was probably the first official laboratory in Africa in Nigeria early in 1961. The writer joined them late that year.

George Soloyanis,[5] who was one of the staff members in the 1961-64 series, continued to develop and present workshops in Ghana, Nigeria, and Egypt in 1964, 1966, and 1967 for business and educational organizations. One was for the Ghana Diamond Mines at the behest of a participant of a prior workshop. Several were conducted for the Shell Oil-British Petroleum (Shell-BP) Company of Nigeria, and they had planned others when the Biafran-Nigerian civil war broke out and caused the plans to be canceled.

Shepard Insel,[6] a Ford Foundation-supported education and training consultant in Nigeria in 1965-67, also worked with Shell-BP. Among the workshops he helped to design and implement was a one-week lab used as an introductory experience to a three-week training course. The goal of the course itself was to further prepare Africans who would be taking over the reins of the company from the expatriates. The goal of the lab was to facilitate building of better relations between the Africans and the Europeans. Here again, as in the VTTE seminar, the laboratory was used as a way to facilitate subsequent structural, technical content learning.

Though most of these workshops were staffed by men who knew, or knew of each other, there was one series held in Africa, starting in 1962, that few heard about. This series was supported by the Episcopal Church of the United States and the Anglican Church of England. The aim was to train Africans within the Anglican church to become trainers to work within the church. These individuals were to function as agents of change; that is, to become the prime movers in an effort to bring about greater understanding and cohesiveness among the members of the Anglican church. They were also to be the rallying points for parishioners' efforts to modernize and to make more meaningful and relevant the teachings of the church to the problems in the Africa of today.

David G. Jones[7] was the architect of this lab series, and he held workshops in Liberia, South Africa, and Uganda. In one instance his colleague, Don Griswold (currently with the University of Buffalo), held a workshop in Zululand (South Africa) under the auspices of the Anglican church. What made it especially note-worthy was that the workshop was ecumenical and the participants multiracial. There were two bishops in this workshop, one black and one white, one African and one English. Though there were protests, the workshop was counted a success.

An Egyptian workshop series took place in late 1966 and 1967. This was presented primarily by and for the Egyptian National Institute of Management Development. The series consisted of four management-development laboratories (basically sensitivity training). One was a two-week lab, the remainder lasted one week. Uniquely, one of these labs was a "family" lab—that is, a sensitivity-training-based workshop in which an organization's manager and those reporting to him are the participants. To the writer's knowledge, no other family labs were presented in Africa, and few of them have been held in the United States. Staff for these labs was drawn from several sources. R. K. Ready[8] and Donald King[9] were Ford Foundation consultants and were based in the Egyptian National Institute of Management Development. George Soloyanis was with the Ford Foundation in Cairo and helped design and staff the labs. Shepard Insel was another staff member of one of the labs, flown in from Nigeria. In this series a definite attempt was made to help develop Egyptian nationals for later training activities. Fouad Sherif and Esmat Magorgi, both Egyptian nationals, functioned as junior staff members late in the series.

It is interesting to note that many of the laboratory efforts were staffed by men who were in Africa at the time, some thousands of miles from each other, who were qualified to staff workshops. Often they came together as a team to present the workshop on very short notice. The Ford Foundation frequently pulled the staffing for their workshops from such diverse locations as Kampala, Uganda; Enugu, Nigeria; Accra, Ghana; and Nairobi, Kenya. These men would meet several days before the actual workshop and design it for the anticipated participants, the location, and the articulated goals. In almost all cases the staff members had another job in their "back-home" African nation and were "on loan" from their parent organizations—for example, the Uganda Electricity Board and The Kenya Ministry of Education. It is indicative of the level of support given these workshop efforts that people were released from their positions long enough to participate. Though the workshops were not widely known, many of the African leaders thought well of them and saw in them some hope for helping to solve the human-relations or interpersonal problems in their ministries.

In my estimation it is important to mention the contribution of the Ford Foundation to laboratory training in Africa. Ford was active in many countries in Africa, both north and south of the Sahara. At times the Foundation was accepted more readily than were official representatives of the United States government, with the possible exception of the Peace Corps. Part of the Foundation's good reputation resulted from a clear statement of, and adherence to its objectives, which were: the expansion and improvement of education; the advancement of economic well-being; the strengthening of democratic institutions and processes; the promotion of international understanding and world peace; and the enlargement of scientific knowledge.

The laboratory programs Ford supported in Africa could clearly be classified under the first of the objectives. Laboratory methodology in education is relatively new, however, and it took great perspective and bold-ness to support and cosponsor laboratory-method edu-cational activities. The move is a particularly bold one because it was outside the United States, and it is doubly venturesome in those countries that were ex-British colonies. There teaching methods had been pat-terned after the British system, in which relatively for-mal lecturing plays a dominant role in the teaching and learning process. It would have been the more conserva-tive path to stay with "show-and-tell" thinking than to employ a more participative mode. The Africans often commented (usually unfavorably at the beginning of each workshop, and then more and more enthusiasti-cally as the workshop went on) on the highly participa-tive aspects of the experience-based learning of the workshops.

In all, through 1967, the Ford Foundation had direct-ly supported or participated in at least twenty-five edu-cational-training workshops. All used the laboratory approach to learning, and all were at least three days long, lasting at most fourteen days.

The assertion that laboratory methodology was suc-cessful in producing learning in a rapid, meaningful, effective way is supported in several ways. Perhaps the most thoroughgoing action research aimed at assessing the impact of these workshops was sponsored by Ford Foundation. In his research report on the 1961-64 series, Charles Seashore noted that participants reflected high satisfaction with the results of the workshop, in such ways as "large number of concrete applications, strong regard for the acceptance of the staff of Ameri-cans who conducted the program, a strong desire for further training for oneself and for others in the job setting. . . . [Improvement was most strongly felt in the areas of] interpersonal relationships, communications, administrative skills, and staff teamwork."[10]

Near the conclusion of almost all experience-based workshops or labs participants are asked to complete questionnaires about their reactions to the lab experience. Typically the questions cover almost all aspects of the lab, from the physical arrangements to a comparison of it as a learning experience with all other workshops or seminars the participants have ever attended. Africans gave the workshops extraordinarily high marks as a learning experience time after time after time. African civil-service leaders in some instances demonstrated their positive evaluation of the workshops directly by providing men who were to learn laboratory-training skills as well as the funds to help support them while learning.

It is ironic that many of the Africans who are best equipped to do training are currently in the United States. Others cannot be located: some, because of current military and political crises have dropped from sight; some were in the United States when trouble broke out at home and have not been able to return home. A few are at home, using their training knowledge directly, and others have been promoted out of training activities into other types of work. Although the thought represents a slim hope, it would serve Africa well if she could somehow link these trained people together and use them as a Pan-African training resource.

Certainly the workshops held in Africa made the possibilities inherent in the laboratory approach easier to see insofar as emerging countries were concerned— aiding in the development of communities, easing in-

tertribal conflicts, and so forth. More difficult to visu-
alize and harder to comprehend, yet more important,
was their promise as a way to help accelerate the acceptance of change and cohesiveness and understanding
among hostile groups. It was in this context, and with
this history of laboratory experiences in Africa, that the
Fermeda workshop took place.

Appendix 3. The Parliamentary Group and the T-Group

by William J. Crockett

Although it was not planned that way, the Fermeda workshop offered a contrast between two types of groups—those that follow parliamentary procedure and those that are relatively unstructured and leaderless. In this appendix a contrast is drawn, first between the usual public international conference and Fermeda in general, and then between the General Assembly and the T-groups at Fermeda.

In the typical conference, the head of each delegation is a person prominent in government or in private life; he has the formal rank of ambassador or minister and is supported by substantive and political experts and advisers. Official delegations arrive after intensive briefing by their governments and bring with them formidable documents, some highly classified, called position papers. These papers set forth the official views concerning the problem being negotiated, and they serve as the broad boundaries within which the negotiators may operate. At Fermeda there were no leaders, no staffs, and no position papers. The participants had not been briefed by their governments beforehand; they were not delegates. They came to discuss the border disputes, and they were constrained only by their feelings of loyalty to their countries and by their own understanding of the issues.

In the usual conference there may be a clash over questions of protocol involving seating arrangements, number of advisers who may be present, the selection of a chairman, and the like. At Fermeda no problems of protocol arose until the General Assembly came into existence. Similarly, the delegates to an international conference may wrangle over the agenda, especially for the benefit of representatives of the mass media who may be present: at this point their eyes are on the public rather than on the issues. This exhibitionism we were also spared at our workshop: the participants were impatient to begin a discussion of the disputes, and the project received no-publicity whatsoever.

Usually the head of each delegation makes an opening statement in which the obvious is more or less restated: an attempt is made to anticipate what the opposition will say and to counter those views in advance. The idea, of course, is to put one's antagonist on the defensive. At Fermeda we had no opening statements and, at least at the outset, no barrages of propaganda.

The leaders of the usual kind of international meeting receive detailed instructions from their foreign offices before they arrive and, as negotiations proceed, between sessions. They say what they have to say; they play the role they are directed to play. Our Fermeda participants were definitely not puppets: the positions they took and defended, and the solutions toward which they groped were their own.

The design for Fermeda called for two T-groups, formed across national lines, that were to meet for about a week in unstructured sessions without agenda. During this time all participants were to come together twice each day in a general session and, of course, for meals, group socials, and recreational activities. One session was to be devoted to the presentation and discussion of theory, and the other to evaluating the progress of the T-groups. But this General Assembly, as the general sessions came to be called, was not intended to be one group; it was envisioned as two T-groups meeting together to accomplish mutual tasks and to accommodate mutual needs. The members were to provide little leadership at the meetings. What leadership they required was to be provided by the trainers, who would conduct the theoretical and evaluative sessions. Once the T-groups had actually developed a group cohesiveness, it was then planned to split up the old multi-country T-groups so they could re-form into country groupings in order to work on the first phase of the problem (to find alternative solutions) and finally to create one large group of the whole (to select one solution upon which all could agree).

After the T-groups had developed a group feeling (by about the third day of the first week), the participants were eager to set to work on the border disputes. But in a meeting called to discuss procedure, the whole group clearly decided that they did not wish to work in *new* country groupings (as we suggested) but instead to return to their old T-groups. The next question was therefore, "How can we draw these two independent T-groups into some kind of common group?"

We, the trainers and the organizers, were of the opinion that a means of melding the two T-groups would be to have one person from each country in each T-group take over the responsibility for planning the ensuing sessions. This was our way of transferring leadership roles to the group, and it was eagerly accepted by the participants.

This planning committee, in developing the agenda, called the total group meetings the General Assembly and decided that these meetings should be run by a rotating chairman, to be chosen by the planning committee each time, and that parliamentary procedures were to be used at these sessions. In retrospect it seems to have been a mistake to permit the general meetings to adopt parliamentary procedure. An even greater mistake was the failure to provide us, the trainers, with a means of intervening in these meetings for procedural reasons except through the cumbersome route of being recognized by the chair.

The General Assembly produced structured meetings that can be contrasted with the unstructured T-groups. The latter—though unstructured with respect to leadership, rules, and protocol—moved to solutions involving the consensus of the total group. Someone would suggest a course of action, and disagreement and compromise would be handled quite quickly. There was wide participation. There was a sharing and an understanding of personal and country needs. There was high mutual trust and esprit de corps. The T-group became a safe, warm, comfortable place where individuals, even though they were nationals of different countries, felt at home and relatively uninhibited. For this reason there was compatibility and harmony. There also was high purpose and commitment within the group to achieve its objective.

The cohesiveness of the T-group was again demonstrated at the end of the first week, when we wanted the participants to move out of their T-groups to form country groups in which to work out solutions for the border disputes. But they refused, saying in effect, "We are happy in our T-groups. There we are accepted. There we are trusted and can give our trust. There we are at home." And there they unanimously elected to remain and to work to the very end of the workshop. It was the belief of the trainers that the T-groups had created warmer, closer multicountry ties than had existed even within the national groups.

Each of the two T-groups developed a plan for settling the border disputes that recognized the deep emotional involvement of the Somalis in the areas. Sacrifices had, therefore, to be made by participants from all three countries in order to achieve a solution that would benefit everyone. A "win-win" frame of reference developed, so that at the end there was genuine commitment on the part of everyone in each group for the plan that emerged.

Since the two proposals differed from each other, they were given to the planning committee, which was asked to make an attempt to integrate them. That committee decided to produce a single document for presentation before the General Assembly. After working most of the night to complete the job, it presented to the General Assembly a unified proposal that, it hoped, would be debated and perhaps adopted.

The reception by that Assembly was definitely not enthusiastic; rather considerable hostility burst forth. In the typical fashion of the formal international conference, there followed speeches for effect, the repetition of arguments, and the reenactment of roles. The participants seemed to be releasing themselves from their earlier commitment to give and take, almost as if they were awakening from a long sleep. And once released, they vigorously attacked the new document in the most blatant and demagogic terms, as if it were not the product of their own invention.

In fact, the General Assembly effectively destroyed both plans, along with most of the commitment to either, and in this process also destroyed the integrated plan of the planning committee. Their product soon succumbed to the unreasoning process of parliamentary procedure.

In the T-group the participants had had a means of understanding each person uniquely: they could begin to appreciate his personal needs and feelings and the ways in which he perceived himself and the problems of his country. But they behaved quite differently when they interacted within the formal structure of a parliamentary system. The old format returned, and there were cries of "Mr. Chairman," "Point of order," "Is there a second?" or "Let's vote on that." Parliamentary maneuvering tended to replace attention to the significant issues and recognition of deep sentiments within others. National feelings came to the fore, and strongly patriotic sentiments were expressed.

In the T-group the members could cope with problems of aggressive behavior, of attempted domination, and of the unbalanced use of speaking time, by means of direct confrontation and open discussion. In the parliamentary process this task fell upon the shoulders of the chairman, who had no means of handling these issues and little evidence of group support when he made the attempt to do so. It was interesting, for example, to see how one person imposed himself upon the entire group. He created real fear and caused the participants to listen to his negative remarks. Somehow he prevented the entire group from breaking out of his grasp.

No decision or action was ever considered irrevocable by the T-groups, but a vote in the General Assembly seemed to settle the matter once and for all. At one meeting, for example, after it was voted to adjourn, someone recalled that an issue affecting the pleasure and comfort of the entire group had been neglected; the decision to adjourn, nevertheless, could not be reversed. "After all," it was stated, "we did vote to adjourn."

In the T-group, in short, each person's mask soon

dropped away, and he became an individual quite separate and apart from the role he played in real life. In the
General Assembly the life roles came back almost immediately, with the person's almost compulsively clutching
his role for protection and comfort. In the T-groups we
had succeeded in having the members look at the issues
as unaffiliated human beings without roles. But they
quickly wrapped their nationalist roles around themselves in the parliamentary session. Several said, "You
have asked me to be an individual, but I'm also a Kenyan [or Somali or Ethiopian], and I must look at my
country's problems that way." Another said, "I can
never agree to a course of action that would give up one
inch of my country's land or one bit or my country's
sovereignty." In this latter instance I felt that the individual's speech made it obvious that his position was
important to him and that he wanted his role understood by his countrymen; therefore, he had the need to
be dissociated from any specific ideas for settlement
that might compromise him later.

We plainly saw at Fermeda that role-induced speeches,
parliamentary tactics, theoretical principles, extreme nationalistic viewpoints, criticism, and polarization—all of
which were part of the parliamentary process—were not
helpful but actually destroyed the effort to find a compromise and to make concessions. On the other hand,
we noted that the very absence of these tactics in the
T-groups did enable them to find solutions agreeable to
all. The intransigence one comes normally to associate
with the international conference was missing in the
T-groups principally, I believe, because the participants
were able to become more personal, less role-inhibited,
less nationalist in feeling, and therefore more reasonable, more cognizant of the total problem, and more
willing to compromise and make concessions.

Appendix 4. Unobtrusive Measures

by Leonard W. Doob and William J. Foltz

The indices listed in this Appendix are ones that we either casually and sometimes unwittingly employed during the workshop or that have occurred to us later upon reflection. We have no way of knowing which ones are practical and which possess validity in terms of the stated objectives. Obviously the mode of implementing them must depend upon the site and the available time. *A warning,* since by definition these measures are employed without informing the participants: some of our African participants at Fermeda told us that they had no desire to be treated as guinea pigs, especially by non-Africans.

    I.   Association across national lines
        A.   National composition of informal groups
            1.   At meals: tables must be small, so that the entire group can break into subgroups; the custom of sitting anywhere must be established from the outset
            2.   During period of relaxation: coffee breaks, partners or opponents in games (card playing, ping-pong, and the like), walks and hikes, drinking in bars and cafes, singing
            3.   During T-group sessions: who sits next to whom
            4.   In public transportation: going to and returning from the site; during the workshop itself (for example, at Fermeda the break between the two weeks involved a bus trip to Venice)

       5. Situations involving expertise: inter-
preting (Italian, which many of the Somalis at Fermeda knew well, as a useful
language), weather prophecy, first aid
- B. Verbal communication
  1. Forms of address, including use of
titles and first names
  2. Use of vulgarity or obscenity
  3. Topics of informal conversations
  4. Rapidity of shift into English for the
benefit of newcomer
- C. Sharing and hospitality: offering cigarettes,
paying for drinks
- D. Physical distance, handshaking, other bodily contact during conversations

II. Acceptance of culture traits from nationals of
other countries
- A. Verbal communication
  1. Use of their technical terms and idio-
matic expressions known previously or
learned during workshop
  2. Use of their proverbs and songs
  3. Attentiveness to news from their country
  4. Appreciation of their forms of humor
  5. Expression of interest in their culture
in any form
- B. Acceptance of their recreational forms and
styles
- C. Direct imitation of anything they do:
clothes, form of eating and drinking, social
behavior

III. Morale of T-groups
- A. Attendance: punctuality, speed of assem-
bling, walking out

    B. Perseveration of T-group problems or discussions when the group is not in session, as indicated in conversations and inquiries

    C. Verbal communication

        1. Ways of referring to the group: use of "we"

        2. Use of forms derived from parliamentary procedure: raising hand for permission to speak

        3. Expressed attitude toward the group

        4. Breaking of taboos while in the group

            a. Social, religious taboos

            b. Political taboos: criticism of own government

        5. Joking and other forms of aggression

IV. Morale of the workshop community

    A. Verbal communication

        1. Ways of referring to workshop

        2. Expressed attitudes

    B. Decisions concerning duration of work and play

    C. Ceremonials: farewell speeches, thank-you notes

    D. Attitude toward tape recorder

    E. General cooperativeness

        1. In games and other exercises

        2. Carrying out instructions of trainers and T-group

Appendix 5. Survey of Reactions

by Leonard W. Doob and William J. Foltz

During the last full day of the workshop all eighteen African participants were given a questionnaire designed originally by Richard E. Walton and amended slightly by the rest of us. Thirteen returned the sheets. We are of the opinion that the five who did not cooperate were probably thus demonstrating their unfavorable attitude (although, of course, the survey was anonymous) and that therefore the figures below err on the favorable side. The tabulations are reproduced to complete the record of Fermeda; the figures represent the number of participants agreeing with the indicated alternative (a sum less than thirteen means that some of the men did not reply or that some of the replies were unclear); except where indicated, each question was followed by a five-point scale; the omission of a category means that no one used it.

1. To what extent do you believe members of the workshop have developed more open attitudes toward possible solutions of the disputes?

       2 very large   4 moderate

       3 large   4 small

2. To what extent have you gained a better understanding of the views of other countries toward the disputes?

       5 very large   8 large

3. To what extent have you become better acquainted with the culture and internal problems of the other countries participating in the workshop?

       3 very large   5 large   5 moderate

4. To what extent do you believe the workshop has produced innovative ideas relevant to solving the problems between Ethiopia and Somalia and between Kenya and Somalia?

    1 very large   4 moderate   6 small
    1 large   1 not at all

5. To what extent did you gain any additional insight into your own communication skills or other aspects of group process?

    1 very large   5 moderate   2 small
    2 large   2 not at all

6. How useful did you find the following aspects of the workshop? *(4-point scale)*

  a. Lecture or theory presentation
    2 very   4 some
    4 moderately 2 little or no

  b. Exercises (squares, disarmament game)
    2 very   2 some
    6 moderately 2 little or no

  c. T-group meetings during first week
    4 very   3 some
    4 moderately 1 little or no

7. Do you have any reactions regarding the following aspects of the workshop? *(open-ended)*

  a. Location
    6 very good   3 too isolated
    1 good   2 English-speaking site preferable

  b. Length of time
    1 very good   3 too short
    4 good   3 too long

  c. Daily schedule
    4 good   1 poor
    1 too long   4 too exhausting or fatiguing

    d. Type of person attending
       3 very good   1 not good
       6 good

8. In your opinion, to what extent did the fact that the organizers and trainers were Americans rather than Africans constitute an advantage or a disadvantage?
       3 very much an   6 advantage and dis-
          advantage   advantage
       3 some advantage   1 disadvantage

9. Compared to other similar seminars or workshops I have attended, I think this has been:
       2 best possible   5 average
       4 above average

10. What—in your own words—did you get out of the workshop? Was it worth the sacrifice you made to participate?

       Ten persons replied, all of whom made a favorable comment. Four indicated a better understanding of the border disputes and three the opportunity to meet nationals of other countries; and one each mentioned increased self-knowledge, appreciation of the viewpoint of others, "better appreciation of African bourgeoisie."

11. Any other reactions you would like to indicate?

       Only six replied, and each said something different. There were references to personal enjoyment, unfavorable financial arrangements, unfavorable criticism of the procedure, a way to improve the procedure, the suggestion that another workshop be held, and a request to be put on the mailing list for publications.

Notes

Chapter 1

1. Kenya Delegation, "Pan African Unity and the N.F.D. Question in Kenya," in *The Ethiopia–Somalia-Kenya dispute, 1960-65,* ed. Carnegie Institute in Diplomacy, mimeographed (Dar es Salaám: University College, 1965), pp. 40-44. Also I. M. Lewis, *The Modern History of Somaliland* (New York: Praeger, 1965); Mesfin Wolde Mariam, *The Background of the Ethio-Somalia Boundary Dispute* (Addis Ababa: Berhanena Selam, 1964); Saadia Touval, *Somali Nationalism* (Cambridge, Mass.: Harvard University Press, 1963).

2. Touval, p. 12.

3. Colin Legum, *Pan-Africanism* (New York: Praeger, 1965), p. 69.

4. Leonard W. Doob, *Patriotism and Nationalism* (New Haven: Yale University Press, 1964), pp. 161-98.

5. William J. Foltz, *From French West Africa to the Mali Federation* (New Haven: Yale University Press, 1965).

6. Legum, p. 46.

7. Thomas M. Franck, *East African Unity Through Law* (New Haven: Yale University Press, 1964).

8. Leonard W. Doob, "Facilitating Rapid Change in Africa," in *Nations by Design,* ed. Arnold Rivkin (Garden City, N.Y.: Doubleday, 1968), p. 352. Parts of the present chapter are derived or quoted from this source.

9. Elihu Katz and Paul F. Lazarsfeld, *Personal Influence* (New York: Free Press, 1955).

Chapter 2

1. Donald J. Nylen, J. Robert Mitchell, and Thomas A. Wickes, "Five Training Institutes in Staff Development and Human Relations Training in West Africa," mimeographed (New York: Ford Foundation, 1961).

2. Thomas A. Wickes, "West Africa: A Problem in Basic Relations" (Paper delivered to the Society for the Advancement of Management, Cincinnati, 1966). I also talked with people in universities and in other settings about the idea and sent a copy of the talk to one United States senator who, I thought, would be interested, but I had no luck.

3. Leonard W. Doob, "Facilitating Rapid Change in Africa," in *Nations by Design,* ed. Arnold Rivkin (Garden City, N.Y.: Doubleday, 1968), pp. 333-86.

Chapter 3

1. James Rennell Rodd, *British Military Administration in Africa, 1941-1947* (London: HMSO, 1948), p. 150.

Chapter 4

1. Leonard W. Doob: "Facilitating Rapid Change in Africa," *Nations by*

Design, ed. Arnold Rivkin (Garden City, N.Y.: Doubleday, 1968), pp. 333-86.

2. These arrangements have succeeded when the decision is being imposed by some stronger party and usually immediately after a war. However, wartime negotiations and concessions have proved less satisfactory, as in the case of the territory granted to Italy south of the Brenner Pass at the expense of Austria. This boundary included many people of German and Austrian nationality within Italy and has been the source of persistent secessionist movements against deliberate attempts to Italianize them.

3. J. R. V. Prescott: *The Geography of Frontiers and Boundaries* (Chicago: Aldine, 1965), pp. 143-44; see also Yash P. Ghai, "Independence and Safeguards in Kenya," *East African Law Journal* 3 (1963): 181-83.

4. Ghai, p. 181.

5. It is interesting to note that the Republic of Somalia attempted to bring about a plebiscite before independence was granted to Kenya. Somalia must have been aware that plebiscites have never really succeeded in solving disputes based on ethnic grounds except where a solution was being imposed by a stronger outside authority.

6. The Arabs who were concerned about their condition put their case and were given constitutional safeguards. See Ghai, pp. 181-83. It would be quite interesting to investigate the extent to which the government of Kenya has kept its promise in this case, because it might be important as a demonstration for the Somali population in Kenya.

7. Saadia Touval, *Somali Nationalism,* (Cambridge, Mass.: Harvard University Press, 1963), p. 153.

8. See *1962 Kenya Population Census.*

9. Prescott, pp. 144-146.

10. Ghai, p. 183.

11. Ghai, p. 184.

12. Prescott, p. 144.

13. George W. Keeton, *The Passing of Parliament* (London: Benn, 1952), p. 185. Also Richard Rose, *Politics in England* (Boston: Little, Brown, 1964), p. 43.

14. M. G. Smith, "The Sociological Framework of Law" (unpublished ms.), p. 4.

15. "Pan-African Unity and the N.F.D. Question in Kenya," a memorandum presented to the African Summit Conference, Addis Ababa, 1963, by the Kenyan delegation of Oginga Odinga, Mbiyu Koinange, Dr. Gikonyo Kiano, and others.

16. Hans J. Morgenthau, *Politics Among Nations,* (New York: Knopf, 1954), p. 290.

Chapter 6

1. "The Fermeda Workshop: A Different Approach to Border Conflicts in Eastern Africa," *Journal of Psychology* 73 (1969): 249-66.

Chapter 7

1. Harold H. Kelley and Charles K. Ferguson, "Significant Factors in Overevaluation of Own-Group's Product," *Journal of Abnormal and Social Psychology* 69 (1964): 223-28.

2. Leland Powers Bradford, Jack R. Gibb, and Kenneth D. Benne, *T-group Therapy and Laboratory Method* (New York: Wiley, 1964); Edgar H. Schein and Warren G. Bennis, *Personal and Organizational Change Through Group Methods* (New York: Wiley, 1965); Charles K. Ferguson, "Management Development in Unstructured Groups," *California Management Review* 1 (1959): 66-72.

Appendix 2

1. Ford Foundation, Danish Board for Technical Cooperation with Developing Countries, and Swedish Authorities, "Seminar on the Development and Organization of Vocational Training and Technical Education" (Denmark: undated, about 1966).

2. Much of this information is available in Ford Foundation et al., "Seminar." Other facts came to my attention through J. Anthony Stout, Donald Nylen, and M. Host, who were on the VTTE staff.

3. Manager, Personnel, Westinghouse Learning Corporation, Bladensburg, Maryland. Personal communications, 1969.

4. Organization Development Consultant, Gunnar Hjelholt Consultants, Copenhagen, Denmark. Personal communications, 1969.

5. Deputy Commissioner of Mental Retardation, Commonwealth of Pennsylvania, Department of Public Welfare, Harrisburg, Pennsylvania. Personal communications, 1969.

6. Dean, Educational Services and Professor of Psychology, San Francisco State College, San Francisco, California. Personal communications, 1969.

7. David G. Jones. Partner, Jones & Byrd, Inc., Minneapolis, Minnesota. Personal communications, 1970.

8. R. K. Ready. "Introductory Human Relations Training in the United Arab Republic," unpublished manuscript, Cairo, 1965. Also personal communications with Dr. Ready, who is currently at the Center for International Development, NTL Institute for Applied Behavioral Science, Washington, D.C.

9. Professor of Administrative Science and Psychology, Krannert Graduate School, Purdue University, Lafayette, Indiana. Personal communications, 1969.

10. Charles Seashore, "An Evaluation of Staff Development and Human Relations Workshops by the Ford Foundation in West Africa, 1961-63," mimeographed (Washington, D.C., 1965), pp. 1, 2.